Christmas Tree Ornaments

Christmas Tree Ornaments

LORRAINE BODGER

Illustrated by Lorraine Bodger

Sedgewood® Press

AUTHOR'S ACKNOWLEDGMENTS

I would like to express my gratitude to the
following generous and cooperative suppliers:

Wrights Home Sewing Company, for providing
an inspiring variety of high quality
ribbon, rickrack, fringe, lace and other trims.
American Tree Company, for the handsome trees
and wreaths seen in the photographs.
Silvestri, for providing dozens of strings of lights
for the Christmas trees.

FOR CBS INC.
Editorial Director: Dina von Zweck
Project Coordinator: Ruth Josimovich

FOR SEDGEWOOD® PRESS
Editorial Director: Elizabeth P. Rice
Associate Editor: Leslie Gilbert
Production Manager: Bill Rose

Designer: Betty Binns Graphics
Photography: Robert Epstein

ISBN: 0-02-496740-8
Library of Congress Catalog Number 84-52753
Manufactured in the United States of America.

Introduction

Christmas is, of course, a religious holiday; it is also an especially beautiful one. The world is transformed in December: it is illuminated by candles and strings of twinkling lights and decked in red and green. There are wreaths on our doors, Santas on every corner and joy in the air. We anticipate exciting things that happen only at Christmastime— family get-togethers, special meals, music and gifts that remind us of the meaning of this holiday.

Perhaps best of all, we bring home the Christmas tree. It is a tradition we love for its past and present beauty, for the memories it evokes and as a symbol of regeneration. Boxes of lights and balls and other decorations come out of their year-long hibernation and the magic begins.

I would like to think that making the ornaments in this book will enrich your Christmas and that this year, next year and every year after, the ornaments you make will give you pride and joy in your creativity. Merry Christmas!

Lorraine Bodger

Contents

1
Decorating the Tree

Chapter 1 is divided into *Part 1: Basic Tree Trimming* and *Part 2: Techniques and Materials.* Part 1 will help you create a picture-perfect tree by introducing some new ways of thinking about the old basic lights, garlands and ornaments.

Part 2 is a little different. Although almost everything you need to know about techniques and materials is provided right on the page with each project, there is some general information that takes too much space or pops up too often to be explained over and over again. That information is gathered in Part 2.

Part 1: Basic Tree Trimming

LIGHTS

There's nothing like the magic moment when you first turn off the living room lamps and see your very special Christmas tree twinkling with tiny lights.

When choosing lights remember that white ones generally act as a quiet, hospitable background to the ornaments while multi-colored lights have more personality and are likely to become an element in the design of your tree. If your ornaments have a strong theme, like the Victorian Ornaments in the photograph on page 22, you will not want to distract the eye with multi-colored lights. On the other hand, the Children's Ornaments on page 90 have a playful quality that is set off by multi-colored lights.

The color of your ornaments plays a part in the choice of lights, too. A predominantly blue and silver tree, like the one on page 80, would clash with multi-colored lights. The lights should enhance the design of your tree, not compete with it.

GARLANDS

Garlands can be a very effective unifying element when you string them all around the tree in graceful loops. Let the garlands serve as a background—drape them over the branches several inches in from the tips, leaving the tips free for the ornaments.

The garland you choose depends on the style of your tree and the amount of time and money you can spend.

1 Make the garland yourself: The Mexican Garland, page 134, and the Popcorn and Cranberry Garland, page 47, are easy and inexpensive. The Paper Chains, page 113, are an old stand-by with a new twist.

2 Use something unexpected: Try a continuous string of pompons, as seen on the tree on page 66. Ball fringe or brush fringe would also be fun.

3 Buy garlands at a 5-and-10, department store or specialty shop: Gold and silver garlands are good choices because they look luxurious and reflect the sparkling lights on the tree. Long-bristled metallic garlands are always available and sometimes you can find short-bristled garlands too, like the ones I used doubled up on the Folk Art tree on page 122.

ORNAMENTS

In this book I generally give instructions and a materials list for making one of each ornament, but as you can see in the photographs I like to hang at least four or five of each ornament. Once you start gathering the materials for a single ornament, you'll probably have enough for several, and once you learn how to make a single ornament, you'll find it easy to make multiples. In the long run it's a saving of time and money and—more important—the ornaments are far more effective when there are four, five or six of each.

When you decorate your tree, your one-of-a-kind handmade and heirloom beauties should receive pride of place at the tips of the central branches. When you hang the multiples, there are three possible approaches:

1 Distribute them evenly over the entire tree: This works well when the tree is small (5½ feet tall or less) like the tree with Natural Ornaments on page 148. It is also appropriate when there is a predominant color like the red of the Old-Fashioned Country Ornaments on page 42 or when there are a limited number of ornament designs used, like the Scrapbasket Ornaments on the tree on page 80.

2 When you have playful, amusing ornaments in a profusion of bright colors, distribute them randomly over the entire tree: the tree with Children's Ornaments, page 90, and the tree with Folk Art Ornaments, page 130, are good examples of this approach. Remember: *don't* try to tame these ornaments with orderliness; *do* use lots and lots of ornaments so the tree looks deliciously plump and crowded.

3 On a large tree keep each group of multiples confined to a specific area: Take a close look at the Victorian Ornaments on the tree on page 22. If you're sharp you will see that in general the Doily Fans and Rickrack Hearts are on the top third of the tree, the Golden Cornucopias and Crocheted Snowflakes are in the central area and the Eyelet Wreaths and Satin Butterflies cover the lower third. Other ornaments are placed carefully around these ornaments.

On a large tree like this, grouping the ornaments so that your eye takes in several of the same ornament at one time is pleasing; if you scatter the ornaments, you can see none of them clearly and it becomes visually confusing.

TINSEL

To some folks no tree is complete without the final application of tinsel, strand by strand. I feel that the ornaments are the stars of the show—especially if they are handmade by a devoted craftsperson—and the tinsel just distracts the eye from the beauty of the ornaments.

FINISHING TOUCHES

After you have hung all your ornaments, you may still find that you have some unattractive bare spots which need to be filled in. Consider the following possibilities in keeping with the style of your tree.

1 **Christmas balls:** The obvious choice, but give some thought this year to the sizes, shapes and colors you choose. Avoid the oversized, the bizarre and the clashing.

2 **Garlands:** When the tree is completely decorated it may be too late to add a whole garland, but you can cut a store-bought garland into small pieces and tuck the bits into the bare spots. Metallic gold or silver bits will reflect the lights and look quite twinkly and pretty.

3 **Bows:** First cut some $\frac{3}{4}''$-$1''$ wide apparel ribbon (perhaps a double-face satin or a dotted grosgrain) into 24" pieces. Then tie

each piece of ribbon to a branch and make a graceful bow. This is expensive the first year you do it, but the ribbon can be reused for many years. If you can't afford real ribbon, the next best choice is wide satin-finish gift wrap ribbon. In either case, put lots of bows on the tree because a few scattered bows will just look silly.

4 Pinecones: Make Frosted Pinecones (page 150) and attach them all over the tree in pairs.

5 Dried flowers or fabric flowers: Small bouquets tied with ribbon can be charming fillers for almost any style of tree. For example, fabric daisies and cornflowers tied with red grosgrain ribbon would be wonderful on a country-style tree; baby's breath combined with pink and lavender dried flowers, tied with pink satin ribbon, would be per-fect on a more formal or Victorian tree. Tuck the bouquets into the branches or attach them with very thin wire.

6 Small baskets: Tie the baskets to the branches with narrow ribbon or several strands of yarn. If you want to fill each basket, you might put a small block of florist's foam in the basket and push some holly leaves, dried flowers or mistletoe into the foam. Or fill each basket with bits of bright garland, tiny Christmas balls, a yarn pom-pon or small pinecones.

Part 2: Techniques and Materials

HOW TO TRANSFER A PATTERN
TO MAKE A TEMPLATE

The instructions for some ornaments include full-size patterns which must be transferred from the book page to heavy paper or thin board to make sturdy templates. The templates—exact copies of the patterns—can be outlined on fabric or paper as many times as you like to make identical ornaments. The process is simple:

1 Place a piece of tracing paper over a pattern in the book. With pencil or pen, copy the pattern onto the tracing paper.

2 Put a sheet of ordinary carbon paper, ink side down, on a piece of heavy paper or thin board. NOTE: Use a file folder, an index card, a piece of Art Board, poster board, oaktag, etc. Place the tracing paper on top of the carbon paper and draw firmly over the outline with pencil or ball point pen.

3 Remove the tracing and carbon papers and cut out the transferred pattern on the black outline. This cut-out is the template.

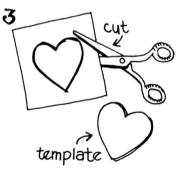

HOW TO WORK WITH WHITE GLUE

White glue—e.g. Elmer's® or Sobo—is a thick, all-purpose liquid glue that dries clear. It is durable, waterproof and long-lasting, though not permanent. It can be used full strength or slightly diluted with a few drops of water. There are several ways of applying the glue:

1 Apply it directly to the ornament, straight from the pointy-tipped plastic container.

2 Pour some into a small dish or paper cup and apply it with your finger, a toothpick, a cotton swab or a paint brush.

3 Pour it into a container, dip an item (for example, a tiny flower) into the glue and set the item in position on the ornament.

If a project does not specify which method to use, choose the one with which you feel most comfortable. Some people just don't like to put their fingers directly into the glue. Other people prefer the control that a paint brush gives.

Keep a pair of tweezers handy when you are gluing very small things like tiny flowers, beads, sequins or little squares of paper. With a tweezers you can pick each piece up and either dip it directly into the glue or hold it firmly while you apply glue to the back of it, then you can place the small item exactly in position on the ornament without a struggle.

White glue, when first applied, is wet and slippery. If you find it difficult to keep two gluey elements anchored in place long enough for the glue to dry and form a bond between them, fasten the two elements together while the glue dries. A spring-type clothespin or a hair clip work best for this job, but a bulldog clip or even a paper clip may help in some cases. Leave the fasteners in place until the glue is dry or almost dry.

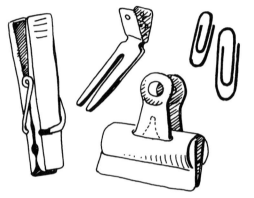

HOW TO TIE A BOW

Many of the ornaments call for a simple, pretty bow that is made from a separate piece of braid or ribbon (any width) and attached with glue. There is an easy technique for making this bow; just follow the step-by-step instructions below.

Remember to keep the loops taut as you knot the center and be sure to make the center knot good and tight. If the ribbon has a right side and a wrong side (like single-face satin ribbon), turn the ribbon when necessary to keep the right side toward you. When the bow is complete, clip the ends in single or double points, following the photographs or drawings for guidance.

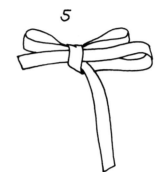

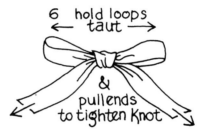

Bend ribbon on dotted lines

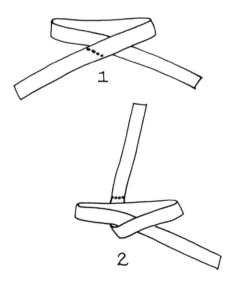

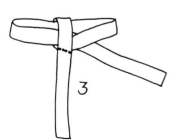

LOOPS FOR HANGING

Loop is the all-purpose term I use to indi-
cate the ribbon, cord, string or wire that
fastens an ornament to the Christmas tree.
As you can see below, sometimes it is loop-
shaped and sometimes it is not.

The loop may be attached to the ornament
by stitching, gluing, tying or some other
method. Every ornament in the book has
instructions for attaching its own particular
loop.

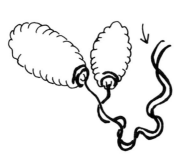

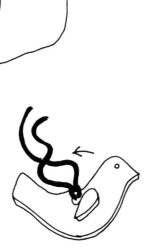

SCORING

If you want to make a perfectly clean, straight fold in a piece of heavy paper or thin board, you must first score it with a sharp blade.

Place a metal ruler on the indicated scoring line. Pressing very lightly into the paper, run a mat knife, X-acto® knife or single-edge razor blade along the ruler to make a cut that just breaks the surface of the paper. Fold the paper on the scored line.

FUSIBLE WEB

Fusible web is a paper-thin sheet of heat-sensitive adhesive used for bonding two pieces of fabric. Stitch Witchery® is the most widely available brand. It is sold in small packages (narrow widths) and by the yard (18″ wide).

The web is cut to size and placed between two pieces of fabric; when a hot iron is applied to one of the pieces of fabric for a certain length of time, the adhesive melts and fuses the two pieces. The manufacturer's instructions included with every purchase explain in detail how to use the web. NOTE: Instructions for individual projects may sometimes call for you to *heat-baste* before fusing two fabrics. This means to touch the hot iron to the upper fabric just long enough for the heat to melt the web slightly and anchor the fabrics and web, without actually completing the fusion.

HEAVY PAPER AND THIN BOARD

These are used both for making templates and for making ornaments like the Little House (page 95), the Caterpillar Clown (page 101) and the Paper Snowflake (page 137).

Heavy paper and thin board are stiffer than ordinary writing paper but not as stiff as shirt cardboard or mat board; they are substantial enough to use for templates because their cut edges will stand up to being repeatedly outlined; they are hard to fold unless you score them first; they are flexible enough to be curved into cones and cylinders.

Inexpensive heavy papers include card stock, manila folders, index cards and some artist's papers. Inexpensive thin boards include Art Board, oaktag, tagboard, railroad board and 2-ply Bristol board. All may be purchased in a stationery store, 5-and-10, art supply store or craft and hobby supply store.

POLYESTER STUFFING AND BATTING

Polyester stuffing, sometimes called polyfil, is generally used for stuffing pillows. It comes as a big soft mass packed in a plastic bag. Work with small bits about the size of cotton balls; pull the bits puff by puff from the plastic bag. Be careful not to crush them as you stuff your ornament—the idea is to keep them airy and light so the ornaments will be resilient and plump, not hard and solid.

Polyester batting is a soft, flattish sheet of the same material, folded and rolled to fit in a plastic bag. Try not to stretch it as you work with it; simply spread it out gently, pat out the creases and bumps and cut it carefully.

Polyester stuffing and batting are available at the 5-and-10 and sewing or craft supply stores.

POLYURETHANE

Polyurethane is a liquid sealant used to give a very professional look to several different ornaments made of wood or dough. Good quality polyurethane is available in any hardware store in gloss or satin finishes. Apply it with an ordinary paint brush; it dries in a few hours or overnight to form a tough, durable protective coating.

Don't let polyurethane dry on the brush; when you have finished applying it to the ornament, clean your brush immediately in turpentine and then in soap and water.

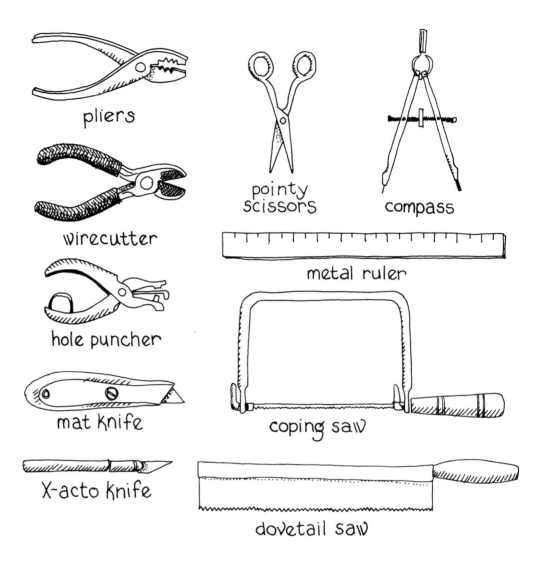

pliers

wirecutter

hole puncher

mat knife

X-acto knife

pointy scissors

compass

metal ruler

coping saw

dovetail saw

A PICTURE GUIDE TO TRIMS

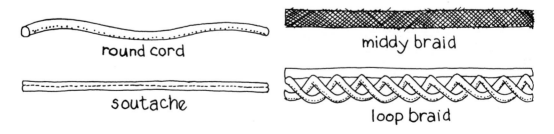

round cord

soutache

middy braid

loop braid

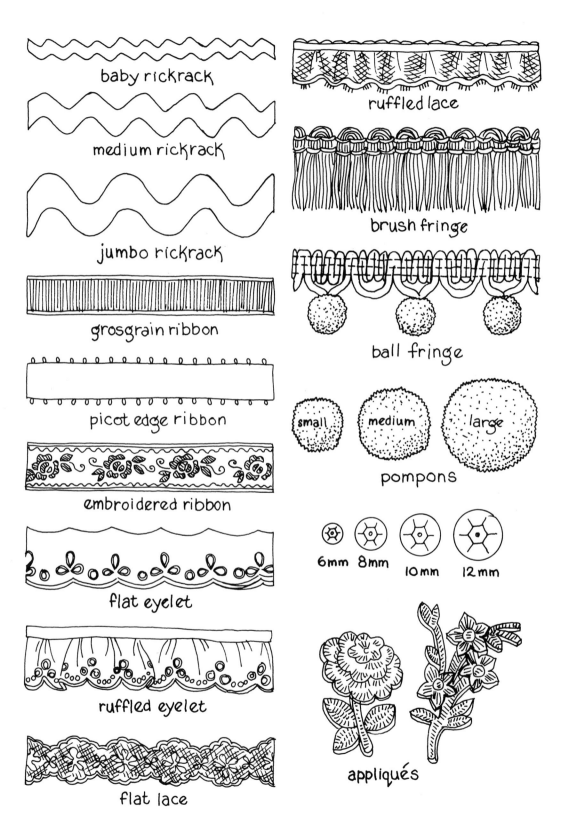

baby rickrack

medium rickrack

jumbo rickrack

grosgrain ribbon

picot edge ribbon

embroidered ribbon

flat eyelet

ruffled eyelet

flat lace

ruffled lace

brush fringe

ball fringe

small   medium   large

pompons

6mm 8mm   10mm   12mm

appliqués

2

Victorian Ornaments

The word Victorian brings to mind ribbons, frills, pastel colors, rich fabrics and a lavish use of gold and silver. To create a Victorian-style tree like the one on page 22 use lots of pastels but temper them with a few deeper accent colors. Vary the textures of the ornaments and introduce plenty of white to keep the tree crisp and clean-looking. White lights are a must for this tree, and bare spots can be filled in with gold and silver balls.

To complete the picture, wrap your packages in matching solid pastels, pastel prints or gold and silver papers and tie them with white ribbons. Or, wrap the gifts in plain white paper and tie them with a variety of pastel ribbons or gold and silver cord.

Satin Butterfly

MATERIALS

Inexpensive satin fabric, 2 pieces, each about 8″ square

Gathered lace, ¾″ wide, one piece 26″ long

Flat cord, ⅛″ wide, one piece 8″ long for the center of the butterfly

Satin ribbon, ⅛″ wide, one piece 8″ long for the loop

Polyester stuffing

1 Transfer the pattern to heavy paper or thin board to make the template as explained on page 15.

Outline the template on the right side of one piece of fabric.

2 Line up the straight edge of the lace with the outline on the satin (right sides together), starting at the lower part of the butterfly as shown in the drawing. Pin or baste the lace in position, making extra little pleats of lace at all the curves. NOTE: These pleats allow the lace to lie flat when the butterfly is turned right side out. Work all the way around to the beginning, overlap the ends and clip off any excess.

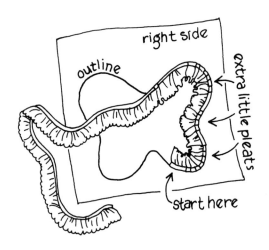

24

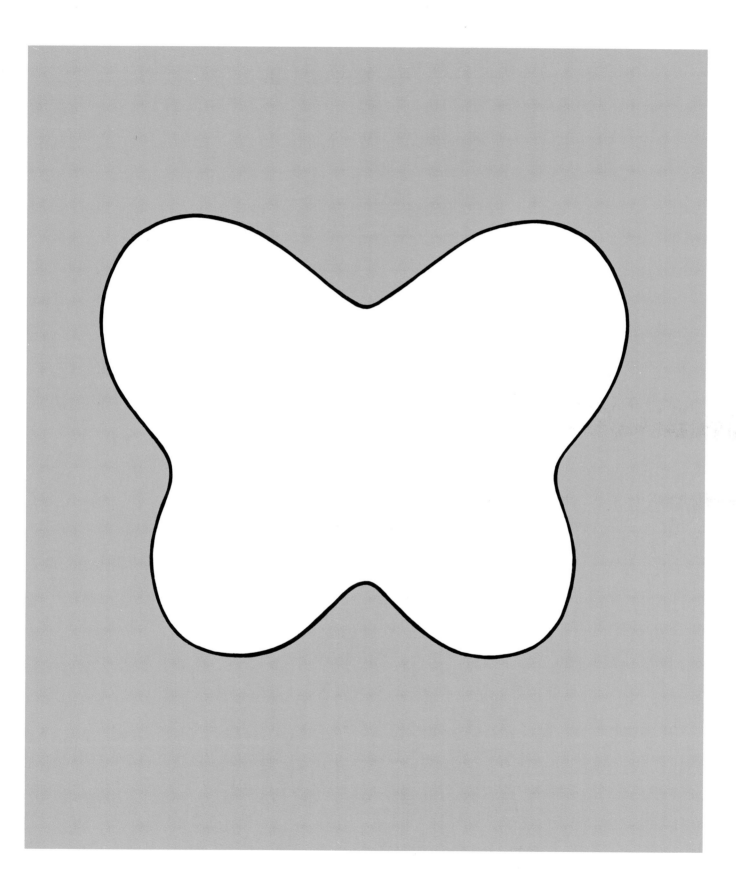

Machine stitch the lace to the satin through the heading of the lace, about $\frac{1}{8}''$ from the outline. Steam iron lightly to set the lace.

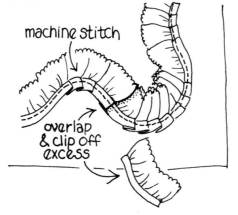

machine stitch

overlap & clip off excess

3 Place the second square of satin on the first, right sides together, and pin. Turn the squares over and stitch together exactly over the previous stitching line, leaving $1\frac{1}{2}''$ un-stitched at the lower edge as shown. Cut off the excess fabric about $\frac{1}{4}''$ from the stitching. Clip the in-curves or trim them very close to the stitching.

right sides together

turn squares over & stitch

$1\frac{1}{2}''$ unstitched

clip

4 Turn the butterfly right side out and iron it carefully, turning under the $\frac{1}{4}''$ seam al-lowances at the opening. Stuff the butterfly lightly and hand stitch the opening closed.

5 Fold the flat braid in half and pin it to the center of the butterfly as shown. Hand or machine stitch the braid through all layers of the butterfly and stuffing.

Fold the satin ribbon in half and tack the ends to the back of the butterfly to make a loop for hanging.

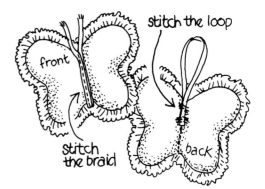

stitch the loop

front

stitch the braid

back

Golden Cornucopia

For an extra treat, top off the cornucopia with pretty candies: fill it about halfway with crumpled tissue paper (so the cornucopia won't be too heavy) and place the candies on top of the tissue.

1 Transfer the pattern (page 28) to heavy paper or thin board to make a template, following the instructions on page 15.
  Outline the template on the wrong side of the gold paper. Cut out on the outline.

2 Glue the loop of the tassel to the wrong side of the cornucopia as shown. Use hair clips to hold the loop in place while the glue dries.

3 Glue lace to the gold side (right side) of the cornucopia. Use your finger to apply glue sparingly to the back of the 5½" piece of lace. Place the piece in position, centered vertically.

Before gluing the 9½" piece of lace around the top edge, make cuts in the lace either between the motifs or about 1" apart, clipping the lace from the lower edge almost to the upper edge.

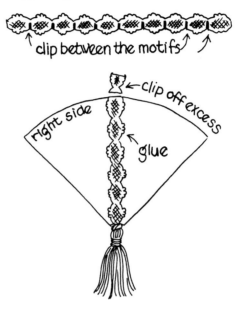

Apply glue sparingly to the wrong side of the clipped lace. Carefully turn the lace over and place it along the top edge of the cornucopia, letting it extend over the top edge about ¼". Pat it down gently, overlapping the edges of the clipped segments so the lace lies flat. Clip off any excess lace at either end. Let the glue dry thoroughly.

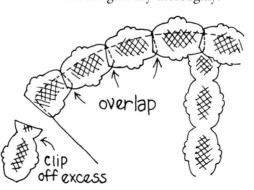

MATERIALS

Heavy weight gold paper, one piece 6″ square

Flat lace, ¾″–1″ wide: one piece 5½″ long for the vertical trim; one piece 9½″ long for the top edge. *Note:* **This lace must have no heading; it should have identical edges, preferably scalloped.**

Flower appliqué

Rayon tassel, about 3″ long with a loop at the top

Velvet ribbon, ¼″ wide, one piece 8″ long for the loop

White glue

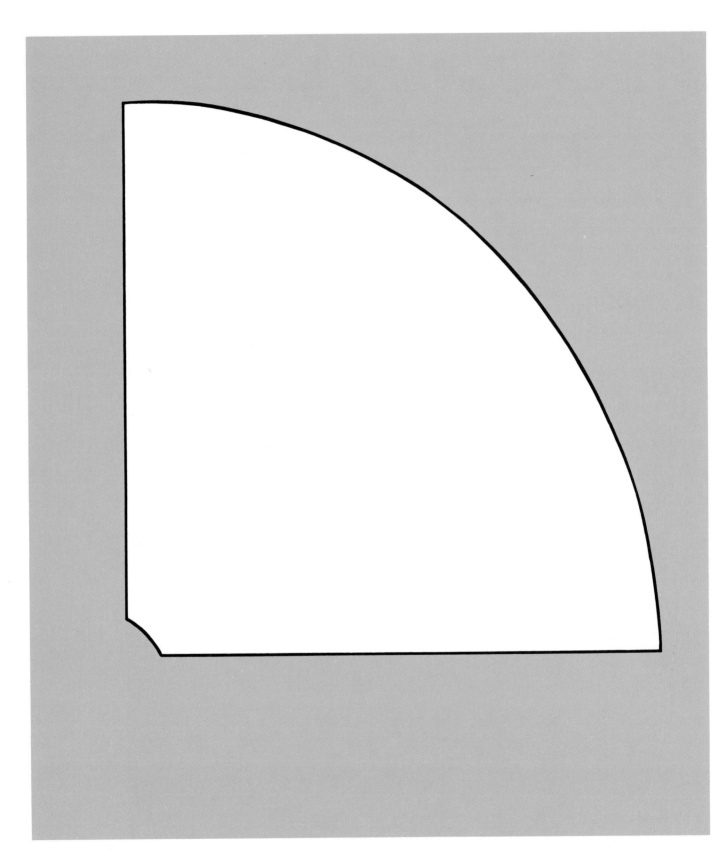

4 Bend and glue the cornucopia into a cone shape. Preset the shape by gently bending the gold paper into a cone. Pay special attention to shaping the narrow end.

Apply glue to the wrong side of one straight edge. Overlap and press the straight edges together in position and hold them until the glue sets. *Tip:* After applying the glue, overlap the upper edges 1″ and secure immediately with one or two clothespins. Then press the rest of the straight edges together and stroke repeatedly to make the glue stick. The lower edges will overlap only about ⅛″.

Clean up any excess glue with a slightly dampened cotton ball. Be sure to dry the gold paper after the clean-up.

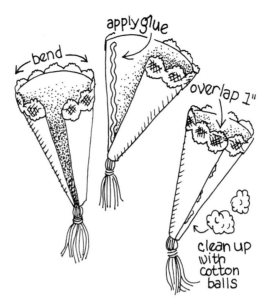

5 Put the finishing touches on the cornucopia, following the color drawing for guidance. Apply glue sparingly to the back of the appliqué and press it in position on the vertical piece of lace.

To make the loop, glue the ends of the velvet ribbon into position opposite each other inside the top edge of the cornucopia.

Eyelet Wreath

1 Fold the raw edge of the eyelet under about 1″ and press. The piece is now 2″ wide and 18″ long. Make a casing by straight-stitching the length of the eyelet ½″ from the fold.

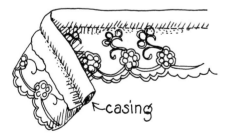

2 Open the loose leaf ring, slip one end of the ring into the casing and gather the entire length of eyelet onto the ring. Close the ring and distribute the gathers evenly around the ring. Steam iron the eyelet lightly to set the gathers. NOTE: You may want to turn under one raw end of the eyelet and tack it over the other raw end with glue or a few stitches.

3 Hold both 13″ pieces of ribbon together as if they were one. Make a bow (see How to Tie a Bow, page 17) and tack it to the wreath, checking the photograph for placement. Trim the ends of the ribbon on a diagonal.

4 Fold the 12″ piece of ribbon in half and tack the folded end to the back of the wreath at the top center edge. Tie the ends of the ribbon to the tree.

MATERIALS

Flat eyelet edging, 3″ wide, one piece 18″ long

Loose leaf ring, 1¼″ diameter

Satin ribbon, ⅛″ wide: 2 pieces, each 13″ long, for the bow; one piece 12″ long for the loop

Doily Fan (page 31), Eyelet Wreath (page 29), Satin Ball with Ribbons (page 32)

Doily Fan

1 Put the gold doily wrong side up on a piece of waxed paper and cover the back sparingly with glue. Center the gold doily glue side down on the white doily and smooth it out gently. Let the glue dry.

2 Cut away one third of the doilies as shown. Fold the remaining two thirds of the doilies in fan pleats. Work in a circular direction using the scallops at the edge of the white doily as guides for folding.

3 Snip off ½" of the folded point. With the sharp needle, puncture a hole through all the layers. Slip the end of the round paper clip through the holes—wiggle the clip gently to force the end through.

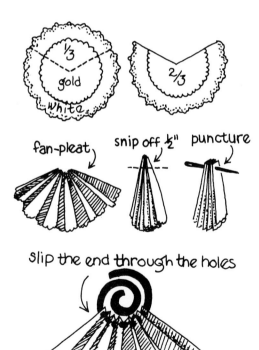

4 With the end of the paper clip on top as shown above, knot the 9" piece of ribbon to the clip at the spot indicated in the drawing below. Tie a pretty bow about 2¼" wide and cut the ends of ribbon on a diagonal.

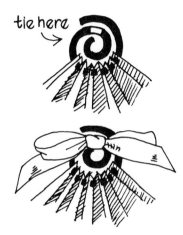

5 Fold the 5" piece of ribbon in half and glue the ends together, clipping them with a hair clip while the glue dries. Turn the fan over to the back and slip the glued ends of ribbon between the top rounds of the paper clip, adding a dab of glue to secure them. Let the glue dry.

6 Clip off each stem close to the flower head. Then dip the back of each flower in glue and place it in position on the fan, checking the photograph for guidance.

Tip: Put the rose in place first, just below and touching the bow, and then tuck the little flowers around the rose.

MATERIALS

Gold paper doily, 4" in diameter

White paper doily, 6" in diameter

Large sharp needle

Spiral paper clip, ¾" in diameter

Satin ribbon, ⅜" wide: one piece 9" long for the bow; one piece 5" long for the loop

5 tiny artificial flowers and one small artificial rose (see photograph, page 30)

White glue

Satin Ball with Ribbons

MATERIALS

Satin ball, 2¾″ in diameter, with plastic loop at the top

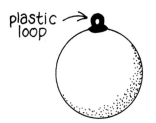

Picot-edge satin ribbon, ⅜″ wide: 3 pieces, each 10″ long, for the ball; one piece 15″ long for the bow

Straight pin

Satin ribbon, ⅛″ wide, one piece about 16″ long for the loop

6-8 tiny artificial flowers plus 2 slightly larger flowers (Cut these from larger bunches or stems of flowers from the 5-and-10 or millinery supply store)

White glue

1 Apply a light film of glue to the back of a 10″ piece of picot-edge ribbon and smooth it around the ball, beginning on one side of the plastic loop and ending on the other. Trim off any excess ribbon if necessary. Repeat with the other two pieces of picot-edge ribbon to divide the ball as evenly as you can in sixths. Let the glue dry.

2 Shape the 15″ piece of picot-edge ribbon into a looped bow as shown in the drawing. Holding the bow firmly, use a toothpick to insert little drops of glue between the layers of ribbon at the center of the bow and on the center back of the bow. Insert a straight pin through the center of the bow. Push

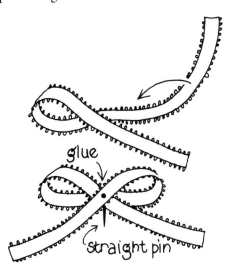

glue

straight pin

the pin into the satin ball so the bow is positioned very close to the plastic loop. Let the glue dry for a few minutes. Trim the ends of the ribbon in points.

3 Clip off each stem close to the flower head. Then, using a tweezers, dip the back of each flower in glue and place it either on the center of the bow or near the bow on the satin ball as shown in the close-up photograph. If there are some tiny green leaves on your flower stems you might like to clip off a couple, dip the stem ends in glue and tuck them into your arrangement. Let the glue dry thoroughly.

4 Attach the loop: Tie the ⅛″ wide satin ribbon to the plastic loop with a double knot. Tie the ends of the satin ribbon to the tree.

double knot

Packages with Paper Appliqués

1 Wrap the small box with pastel gift wrap paper, keeping all pieces of tape on the *back* of the box so they won't show when the box hangs on the tree.

2 Tie the $\frac{3}{8}''$-wide ribbon around the box, knotting it slightly off-center on the front, finishing it with a pretty bow. Clip off any excess ribbon on a diagonal.

3 Cut several flowers from the flower-patterned gift wrap using small, sharp-pointed scissors. Be sure to cut carefully around the flowers, leaving very little background.

Arrange a few paper flowers on the box, using the drawing for guidance. With the small brush, apply glue to the back of each flower. Replace it in position on the box and smooth it down.

4 Slip the $\frac{1}{8}''$-wide ribbon under the wider ribbon on the side or top of the box and tie the ribbon ends to the tree or wreath.

MATERIALS

Small gift box, about $2\frac{1}{4}'' \times 3'' \times 1''$

Solid color gift wrap (Use pastels like pink, pale yellow, light blue, lavender and mint green. If you are making several little packages, consider using one or two more intense colors for accent— deep lavender, brighter blue, rose pink)

Transparent tape for wrapping

Satin ribbon, $\frac{3}{8}''$ wide, enough to wrap around the box and tie in a bow

Gift wrap paper with a pattern of small flowers

Satin ribbon, $\frac{1}{8}''$ wide, one piece 14″ long for the loop

White glue, small brush

Rickrack Heart

1 Transfer the pattern to heavy paper or thin board to make a template as explained on page 15.

Outline the template on the right side of one piece of fabric.

2 Stitch the rickrack across the center of the heart as shown below. The midpoint of the rickrack should be just above the upper point of the heart. Continue stitching the rickrack around the right side of the heart, keeping the rickrack centered on the outline. End the stitching just below the lower point and clip off the excess rickrack.

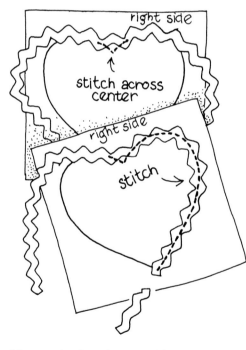

Now go back and repeat this process to stitch the rickrack around the left side of the heart. Iron the stitching to ease out any puckering.

3 Stitch the satin ribbon over the rickrack as shown.

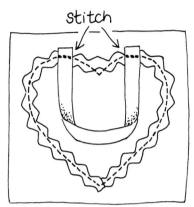

4 Place the rickrack-trimmed fabric over the second piece of fabric, right sides together, and pin. Stitch them together exactly over the previous stitching line, leaving $1\frac{1}{2}''$ unstitched on the straight side of the heart. Cut away the excess fabric about $\frac{3}{8}''$ from the stitching. Clip the fabric almost to the stitching at the top point.

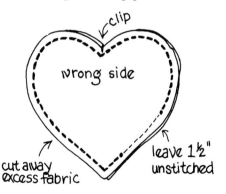

5 Turn the heart right side out and iron it carefully, turning under the $\frac{1}{4}''$ seam allowance at the opening. Stuff the heart lightly and hand stitch the opening closed.

MATERIALS

Cotton or cotton-blend fabric, two pieces each $5\frac{1}{2}'' \times 6\frac{1}{2}''$

Medium rickrack, one piece 18″ long

Satin ribbon, $\frac{1}{4}''$ or $\frac{3}{8}''$ wide, one piece 6″ long for the loop

Polyester stuffing

Crocheted Snowflakes (page 37)

Crocheted Snowflake

The photograph shows snowflakes made by a right-handed crocheter. Lefties can hold a mirror up to the photograph to see how the stitches would look if made by a left-handed crocheter.

Round 1: Ch 8, join last st to 1st st with a sl st to form a ring.

Round 2: Ch 1, 11 sc in ring. Join last sc to 1st st with a sl st.

Round 3: Ch 2, 1 dc in next st, * ch 3, 1 dc in each of next 2 sts. Repeat from * 4 more times to work around ring. Ch 3 and join to ch st with a sl st.

First petal: Without cutting the thread, * ch 4, 1 sl st into next dc, 1 sl st into chain bridge. Ch 6, sl st back into 3rd ch

(NOTE: This 3rd ch will be called *same stitch* from now on.); ch 6, sl st back into same st; ch 6, sl st back into same st; ch 8, sl st back into 6th ch; ch 5, sl st back into same st; ch 6, sl st back into same st; ch 6, sl st back into same st; ch 3, sl st back into same st; ch 1, sl st into same chain bridge; sl st into next dc.

Repeat from * 5 more times to make five more petals. On the last repeat, finish with a sl st into same ch bridge and end off.

Weave in the loose ends and clip off any excess thread close to the crocheting.

Dilute a couple of tablespoons of white glue with just enough water to make the glue a little thicker than milk. Dip the finished snowflake in the solution, soaking it thoroughly. Gently squeeze out the excess liquid. Lay the snowflake on waxed paper and smooth it out to set the shape correctly. Let it dry on the waxed paper overnight or until it is dry on top. Peel it carefully from the waxed paper and turn it over to dry on the other side. Let it dry thoroughly.

Slip one end of the 8″ piece of wire between the threads at the tip of any petal. Attach the snowflake to the tree by twisting the wire around a branch.

MATERIALS

One ball of cotton crochet thread (One ball of Speed-Cro-Sheen makes about seven snowflakes. If you use another thread be sure to choose the appropriate size crochet hook.)

Crochet hook #0

Very thin wire, one piece 8″ long for the loop

White glue

ABBREVIATIONS

st = stitch

ch = chain

sl st = slip stitch

sc = single crochet

dc = double crochet

* = repeat directions following * as many times as indicated

Treetop Ball of Flowers and Streamers

MATERIALS

Styrofoam ball, 4″ diameter

Straight pins

Artificial flowers and leaves: 20-30 large flowers like roses, each about 1½″-1¾″ in diameter; 60-70 small flowers, each about ¾″ in diameter; 15-25 leaves, each about 1″-1¼″ wide and 1½″-1¾″ long

Note: All the flowers and leaves will be purchased in small bouquets or sprays. Unwind the paper that covers the main stem and separate into individual stems. Use a wirecutter to snip off the stem of each large flower, leaving only ¾″ of wire attached. Snip off the stem of each small flower close to the flower. Snip off the stem of each leaf at the base of the leaf.

Satin ribbon, ⅜″ wide: 6 pieces, each 48″ long
White glue

1 Put a pin anywhere in the Styrofoam ball to designate the point at which the ribbons will be attached. When you are gluing the flowers to the ball, leave a clear space around the pin 1″ in diameter.

2 Attach 20-30 large flowers to the ball, spaced evenly over the entire ball: If the stem wire is stiff enough, dip each stem in glue and insert it in the ball. If the wire is not stiff enough, clip each stem off, put a straight pin through a lower petal close to the center of the flower, dip the pin in glue and insert the pin into the ball.

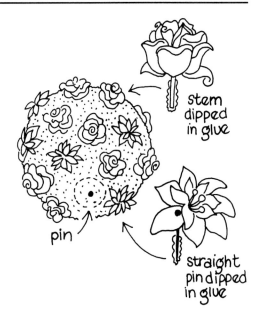

stem dipped in glue

pin

straight pin dipped in glue

3 Attach 15-25 leaves to the ball to fill in the bare spots where the Styrofoam shows between the large flowers. Bend the center wire of each leaf to curve it. Insert a pin at the stem end, dip the pin in glue and push the pin into the ball. You may need several leaves, placed next to each other or overlap-

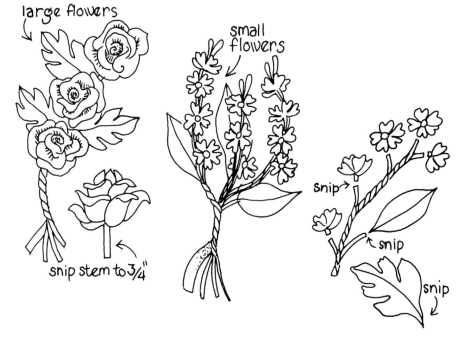

large flowers

snip stem to ¾″

small flowers

snip

snip

snip

Treetop Ball of Flowers and Streamers
(page 38)

ping, to fill in any one bare spot. When you have finished pinning the leaves, there should be very little Styrofoam showing anywhere on the ball.

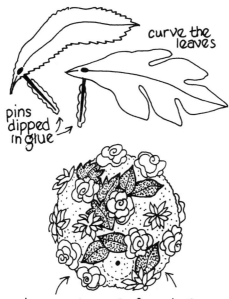

leaves pinned to foam ball

4 Attach 60-70 small flowers in clusters all over the ball to fill out the flower ball and make it look very lush, as well as to cover any tiny spots where the Styrofoam still shows through. Hold each small flower with tweezers, dip the bottom in glue and place it on a leaf or on the Styrofoam (see the photograph on page 39 for guidance). Be sure to tuck some small flowers into any exposed areas around the bases of the large flowers.

Let the glue dry completely.

5 To make the ribbon rosette and streamers, first thread a needle and have it standing by. Fold the first ribbon as shown. Secure it at the center with several small stitches, ending with the needle and thread emerging from the top. Do not cut the thread!

Fold the second ribbon and place it over the first, bringing the needle up through the center of the folded second ribbon. Take a few little stitches to secure the two ribbons. Repeat this process, adding each of the remaining ribbons to the stack, placing them as shown in the drawing to make a rosette shape. When you attach the last (sixth) ribbon you will be making your stitches through 18 layers of ribbon. End off and clip the thread. Trim the ends of the ribbons on the diagonal.

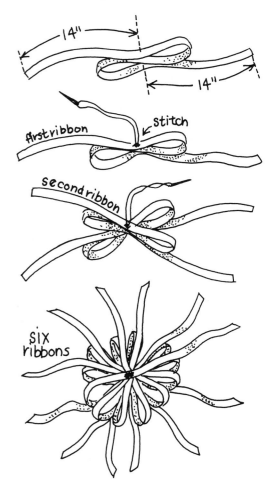

Now push four pins through four lower layers of ribbon, within a $\frac{1}{2}''$ radius of the center stitches—these pins will be used to anchor the ribbons to the flower ball.

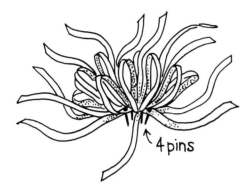

Turn the flower ball upside down, with the pin marker and exposed Styrofoam uppermost; balance the flower ball on some crushed tissue paper so it doesn't roll around. Dab glue on the exposed Styrofoam and on the flowers surrounding it.

Hold all the ribbons and loops away from the four pins. Dab glue on the pins and insert all the pins at once into the exposed Styrofoam area. Let go of the ribbons you have been holding back and press them gently onto the Styrofoam and surrounding flowers. Let the glue dry with the ball and ribbons in this position.

When you place the Treetop Ball on the top of your tree you may want to secure it by hooking some of the ribbon loops over the branches or even by tying two of the ribbons around a branch. If your tree is artificial, bend a few of the top branches into a little nest on which to rest the ball. Spread the streamers out gracefully around the ball and over the top branches.

3

Old-Fashioned Country Ornaments

This chapter invites you to surround yourself with a complete, cozy, homemade Christmas. There are directions for traditional yarn dolls, popcorn garlands and broomstraw stars, as well as two kinds of do-it-yourself gift wraps and a variety of paper patchwork Christmas cards and gift tags. In fact, the gift tags make terrific trimmings for a small tree you can put on a stair landing, in the kitchen or in your bedroom.

You can preserve a beautiful bit of summer by making your own grapevine wreaths. The text and drawings on pages 63–65 tell you how to make the wreaths when the vines are green in August and September, store them through the autumn, and decorate the wreaths when the holiday season arrives.

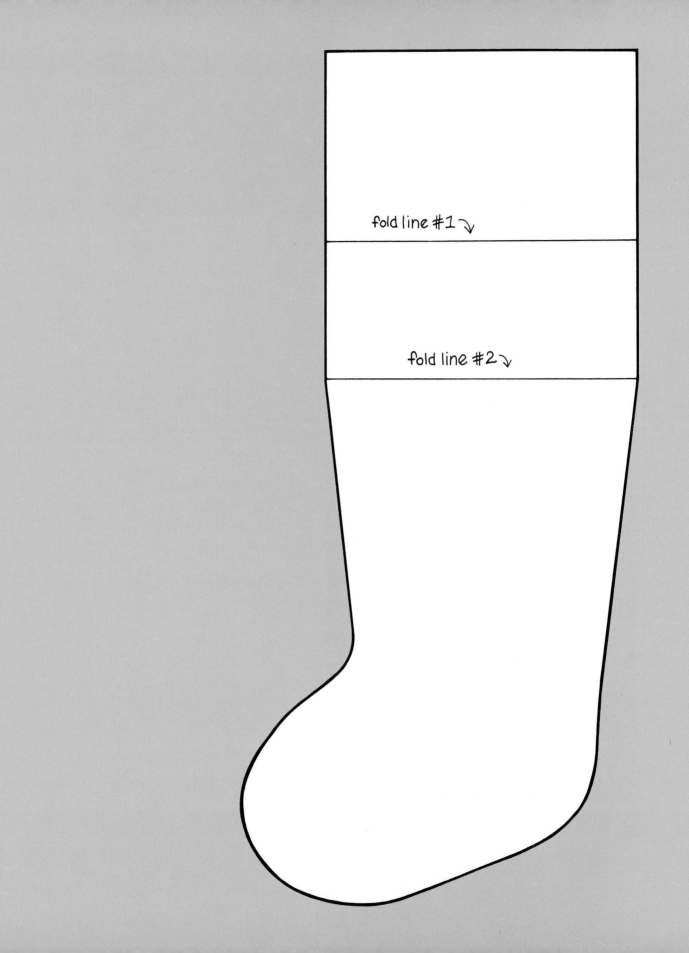

Calico Stocking

1 Transfer the pattern to heavy paper or thin cardboard to make a template as explained on page 15. Be sure to transfer the folding lines, too.

Outline the template on the wrong side of one piece of fabric.

2 Pin the two pieces of fabric right sides together. Stitch them together on the outline *except* across the top. Trim off the excess fabric all around the outline, leaving ¼″ seam allowance.

Turn the stocking right side out and iron. Fold *in* and iron on fold line #1 (see template). Then fold *out* and iron on fold line #2 to form cuff.

3 Fold the ribbon in half and pin the ends 1″ inside the stocking at the back seam. Stitch around the cuff, ¼″ from the top edge, catching the ribbon ends in the stitching. Stitch back and forth over the ribbon ends two or three times to attach them securely.

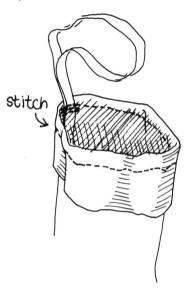

stitch

4 Stuff the stocking lightly with cotton balls or crumpled tissue paper before hanging it on the tree. Top it off by tucking in a bit of gold or silver garland or a small bunch of baby's breath. When you hang the stocking on the tree, knot the ribbon loop to adjust the length if necessary.

MATERIALS

Cotton or cotton-blend fabric, 2 pieces, each 5½″ × 10½″

Grosgrain ribbon, ⅛″ wide, one piece 9″ long for the loop (You may substitute narrow satin ribbon or any flat cord)

Cotton balls or tissue paper

Gold or silver garland or baby's breath

no stitching

wrong side

trim off excess fabric

fold in & iron

right side

fold out & iron

45

Broomstraw Stars

Whiskbroom (the old-fashioned kind made of broomstraws)

Thread

Brightly colored string or crochet thread

White glue

Each star is made up of either five or six bundles of broomstraw. To make one bundle, clip or break 10-12 straws from the whiskbroom; the straws should be about $5\frac{1}{2}''$ long. Hold the straws together and dab a little glue around them about $\frac{3}{4}''$-$1''$ from one end. Wrap thread tightly around the straws, over the glue, several times.

Repeat at the other end of the bundle. When the glue is dry, clip the thread close to the straws.

Make five bundles for a five-pointed star and six bundles for a six-pointed star.

Five-pointed star: Lay out the bundles in a star shape, overlapping the ends at the thread-wrapped points. Carefully pick up or shift each bundle and put a drop of glue at each intersection. Place a heavy book on top of the star while the glue dries.

Six-pointed star: Lay out the bundles in two triangles, overlapping the ends at the thread-wrapped points. Carefully lift each bundle and put a drop of glue at each intersection. Weight each triangle with a heavy book while the glue dries. Then glue the two triangles together with drops of glue at the intersections. Weight with a book again while the glue dries.

Both stars: Tie bits of brightly colored string at each joint—tie a single knot, put a drop of glue on the knot and tie a second knot.

Slip each star right onto a branch of the tree. No loop is needed.

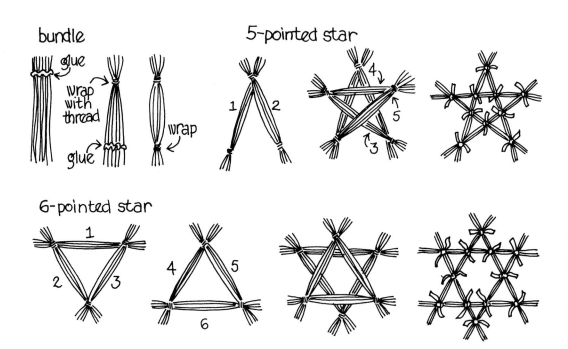

Popcorn and Cranberry Garland

Cut a six-foot piece of crochet thread and tie a fat knot at one end. Put the other end through the eye of the needle. Poke the point of the needle through the center of a square of cardboard and push the square down to the knot. Now string the popcorn and cranberries, either randomly or in a pattern. When the thread is completely filled, poke the needle through another cardboard square, pull off the needle and make a fat knot in the thread close to the cardboard square.

MATERIALS
Popcorn
Cranberries
Thin crochet thread
Large sharp needle
1″ squares of cardboard

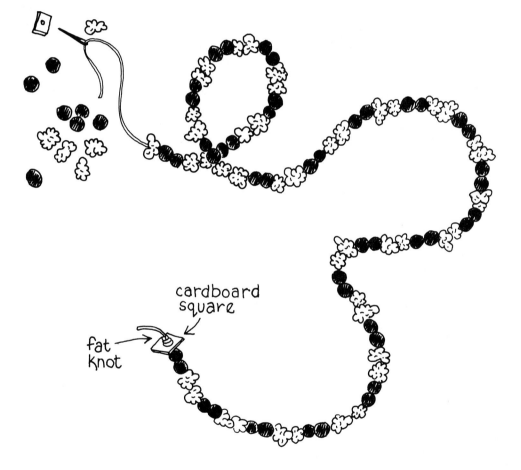

cardboard
square

fat
knot

Yarn Girl and Yarn Boy (page 49), Slice of Watermelon (page 51)

Yarn Girl and Yarn Boy

1 To make either the boy or girl, work with two strands of yarn: Wrap the yarn all the way around the cardboard 20 times; cut the yarn. Then cut a piece of double yarn 15″ long, slip the ends under the wrapped yarn at the top of the cardboard and tie a double knot. This yarn will be the loop; use it to tie the doll to the Christmas tree.

Slip the yarn off the cardboard and cut through the yarn loops at the bottom.

2 Form the neck and head: Wrap a piece of contrasting yarn around the body three or four times as shown and tie a double knot. Put a drop of glue on the knot and tie again. Clip off the excess contrasting yarn close to the knot. NOTE: The side with the knot will be the back of the doll.

MATERIALS

Cardboard, one piece 8″ × 4″

Worsted-weight yarn (The yarn is worked double, so use either two skeins of yarn or wind one skein of yarn into two balls. I used two different colors for the body of each doll: for the boys, light blue plus blue-green or light blue plus medium blue; for the girls, red plus rust or red plus gold. You will also need some contrasting yarn for tying the neck, waist, wrists and ankles)

White glue

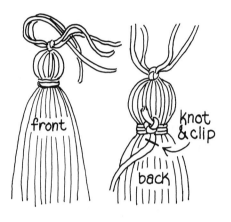

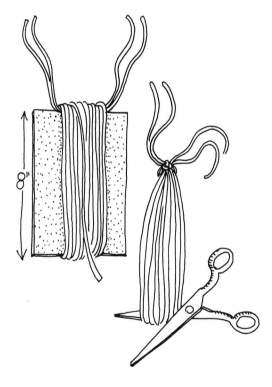

3 Form the waist and arms: Separate 12 strands of yarn from each side of the body. Tightly wrap a piece of contrasting yarn around the body six or eight times as shown and tie a double knot at the back of the doll. Put a drop of glue on the knot and tie once more. Clip off the excess contrasting yarn close to the knot.

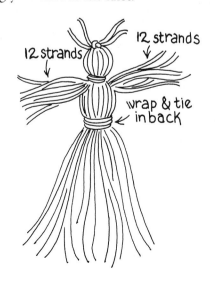

To make one arm, divide one set of 12 strands into three groups of four strands each. Braid the three groups. Tie off the arm 1¾″ from the body, using contrasting yarn, making the knots at the back as described above. Unbraid the arm back to the contrasting yarn and clip off the excess to leave a "hand" about ½″ long. Repeat this process to make the second arm.

4 Complete the doll either as a boy or girl: For the girl, simply trim the yarn skirt to be 3″ long. For the boy, make legs by first dividing the skirt strands in half. Divide each half into three groups of yarn and braid.

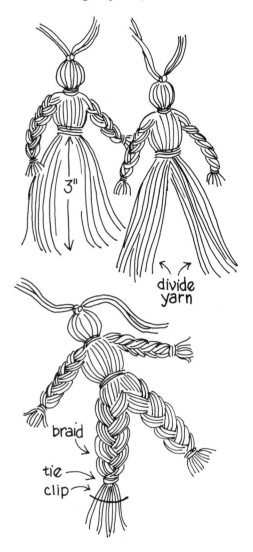

Tie off each leg about 2½″ from the waist, using contrasting yarn, making the knots at the back as described in steps 2 and 3. Unbraid each leg back to the contrasting yarn and clip off the excess to leave a "foot" about ¾″ long.

Slice of Watermelon

1 Transfer the two patterns (page 53) to thin board or heavy paper to make templates as explained on page 15. Be sure to transfer the dotted line on Pattern #2 to the template.

2 Make the front of the watermelon: Outline Template #1 on one piece of green felt; do not cut out. Outline Template #2 on the red felt (remember to transfer the dotted line) and cut out.

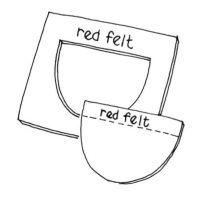

Place the red felt on the green felt, centered as shown, lining up the dotted line with the straight line. Slip a scrap of fusible web between the two pieces and fuse firmly according to the manufacturer's instructions. With white thread zigzag-stitch around the curved edge of the red felt.

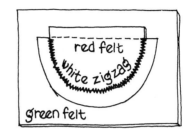

Cut out seven black felt triangles and glue them to the red felt, using the photograph for guidance.

MATERIALS

Green felt, 2 pieces, each 4″ × 6½″

Red felt, one piece 3½″ × 5″

Scraps of black felt

Grosgrain ribbon, ⅜″ wide, one piece 7″ long for the loop

White, green and red thread

Small scrap of fusible web

Polyester stuffing

White glue

3 Place the two pieces of green felt together with the red felt on top. Zigzag stitch with green thread along the straight and curved outlines exactly as shown. Trim away the excess green felt around the curve only, cutting very carefully just outside the stitching.

red thread, zigzag stitch across the red felt at the top edge, catching the ribbon in the stitching as shown. Carefully trim away the felt above the stitching line, leaving the ribbon loop.

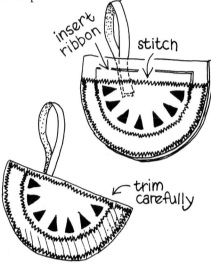

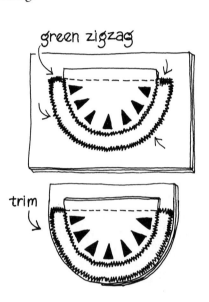

4 Stuff the melon sparingly with polyester stuffing. Fold the ribbon in half and insert the ends into the melon, making sure they reach about $\frac{3}{4}''$ below the top edge. With

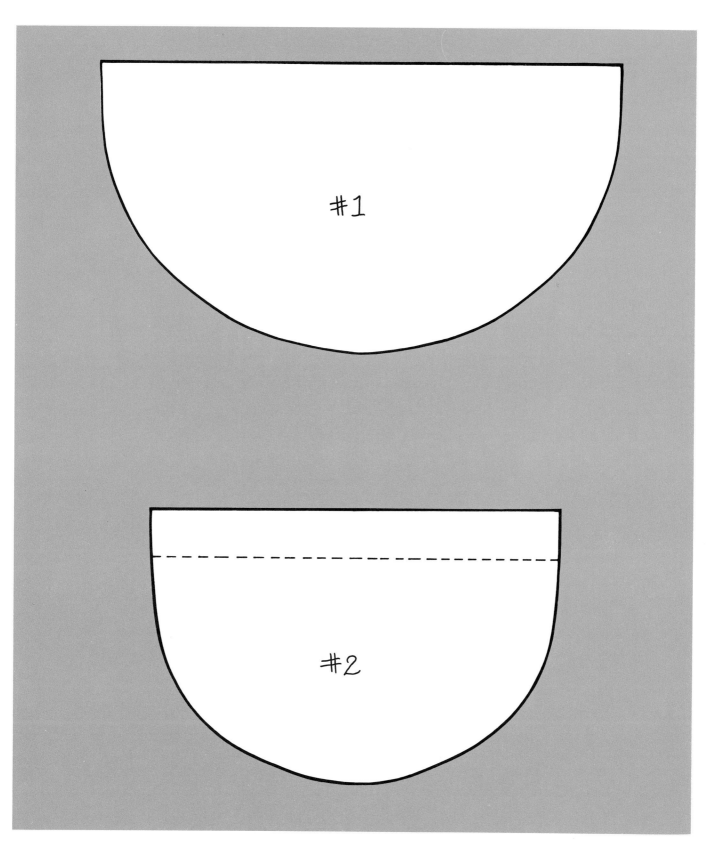

#1

#2

Spatter-Print Gift Wrap

Jars of acrylic tempera paint in one or more colors *Note:* **White, red, blue, green and yellow will give you many possible color combinations.**

Inexpensive paint brush, $\frac{1}{2}''$-$\frac{3}{4}''$ wide

Disposable containers or bowls, e.g., clean plastic yogurt or margarine tubs, plastic-coated paper picnic bowls, clean tuna fish cans

Brown wrapping paper (also called kraft paper), available in wide rolls at a stationery store, card shop or 5-and-10 (Another good choice is inexpensive, matte-finish shelf paper from the 5-and-10. Shiny or glossy paper is *not* suitable)

The photograph on page 55 shows two different types of gift wrap you can make quite easily—spatter-print paper and sponge-print paper. Packages #1, #2 and #7 (see diagram) are wrapped with spatter-print papers.

1 Spread newspaper on the table, floor and any surface likely to be hit by flying drops of paint. Set out a small pitcher of water for mixing with the paint and a jar of water for rinsing the brush. Have paper towels on hand for spills.

2 Shake each jar of paint to mix it thoroughly. Pour an inch of paint into a disposable container and dilute it with water to the consistency of fruit juice, stirring it briskly with the brush. Repeat this process for all the colors you need. If you want to create new colors (for example, pink made by combining red and white), mix the undiluted paints first, get the colors right and then dilute to the correct consistency. NOTE: Remember to rinse your brush in clean water before dipping it in any new color.

Mix and/or dilute all the colors you need before beginning the spattering.

3 Unroll the brown paper and cut off a piece. (The length of the piece is up to you. It depends on the size and number of the gifts you want to wrap.) Spread the paper on newspapers on the table or floor. *Tip:* If the paper starts to curl up, weight down the four corners securely.

4 Dip the brush in paint, hold it about one foot above the brown paper and strike the brush sharply with your other hand. Drops should spatter wildly over the paper. If they don't spatter, either you did not have enough paint on the brush or you did not strike the brush with enough force. Continue spattering until you achieve the coverage you like. Let the paint dry thoroughly.

If you want to spatter two or more colors, let each color dry before adding the next to keep the colors bright.

Spatter-Print (page 54)
and Sponge-Print
(page 56) Gift Wraps

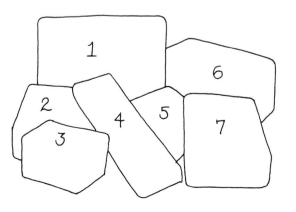

Sponge-Print Gift Wrap

MATERIALS

Solid color gift wrap in rolls (High-gloss papers are not suitable for this project. Use matte-finish or slightly glossy papers)

Jars of acrylic tempera paint in one or more colors (If your paper is white, any of the bright colors will look very festive when sponged on. If your paper is a bright color, white paint is a good choice for sponge-printing)

Cellulose sponges

Disposable plastic-coated paper plates

Packages #3, #4, #5 and #6 in the photograph and diagram on page 55 are wrapped with different varieties of sponge-print paper.

1 Spread newspaper on a large table. Keep a roll of paper towels within easy reach.

2 Unroll the gift wrap and cut off a piece. Remember that the length of the piece depends on the size and number of the gifts you want to wrap. If the paper curls up, weight the four corners securely.

3 Dampen a sponge and squeeze out excess water. Cut the sponge into a piece about $1\frac{1}{2}'' \times 2''$ and cut that piece into a rough oval.

Shake a jar of paint to mix it thoroughly and pour a little puddle of paint into a paper plate. Dab the flat side of the sponge into the paint lightly and then pat the sponge around the plate to remove the excess paint. The paint should be tacky on the surface of the sponge, not gloppy and thick. Pat the sponge on the gift wrap, pressing down slightly to leave a print of the sponge on the paper. Repeat this pat-and-press technique all over the paper, with each new print just touching the previous one. Cover the entire paper with sponge prints. Let the paint dry thoroughly.

There are many variations to try. For example, use two or three colors: print the first color randomly over the paper, print the second color adjacent to the first and then use the third color to fill in all the blank spots. Or work in a geometric pattern: print a row of red, then a row of green, a row of blue and a row of yellow and repeat across the paper.

Paper Patchwork Christmas Cards

Cut a 10″ square from each gift wrap. Staple several of these squares together at one edge and draw a $\frac{1}{2}$″ grid on the back (white side) of the bottom sheet. Cut through all the layers of the stack on the grid lines to make $\frac{1}{2}$″ squares.

Arrange little squares on the front of a blank card, following the designs in the photograph or inventing your own. When the design is complete, lift each square, dab a bit of glue on the back and replace it in position on the card. Let the glue dry and then press the card overnight under a heavy stack of books.

MATERIALS

Gift wrap in country prints, geometrics, solids

Blank cards with matching envelopes (At the stationery store or art supply store you can buy specially packaged blank cards and envelopes made of good heavy paper, just right for creating your own Christmas greetings)

Ruler, scissors, stapler

White glue

1 cut 10″ squares   2 staple   3 draw grid & cut

back

4 arrange squares   5 glue   6 press

Paper Patchwork Christmas Cards (page 57),
Paper Patchwork Mini-Cards (page 59),
Woven Hearts (page 61)

Paper Patchwork Mini-Cards

These little cards make pretty ornaments for the tree and colorful gift tags for packages wrapped either in solid color paper or in one of the papers used in the patchwork.

Score the white paper across the middle and fold it on the scoring line to make a card $2\frac{1}{2}''$ square (see Scoring, page 19).

Cut the gift wrap into $\frac{1}{2}''$ squares. Only a few squares are needed for each card, but cut more than you need so you can play with the colors and design. Cut some of the squares on the diagonal to make triangles.

Arrange the little squares and triangles on the front of the card, following the designs in the photograph or inventing your own. When the design is complete, lift each square, dab a bit of glue on the back and replace it in position on the card. Let the glue dry.

Punch a hole (through both layers of paper) in the upper left corner of the card and slip the string or cord through the hole to make the loop. Tie the ends of the string either to the tree or to the ribbon of a gift-wrapped package.

MATERIALS

Heavy white paper, one piece 5″ × 2½″ (Choose an artist's paper with a slight texture. The salesperson in any art supply store or craft store will be able to recommend something appropriate. Be sure to pick a paper that can be folded crisply)

Gift wrap in country prints, geometrics, solids

Ruler, scissors, hole puncher

String, cord or thin crochet thread, one piece 16″ long for the loop

White glue

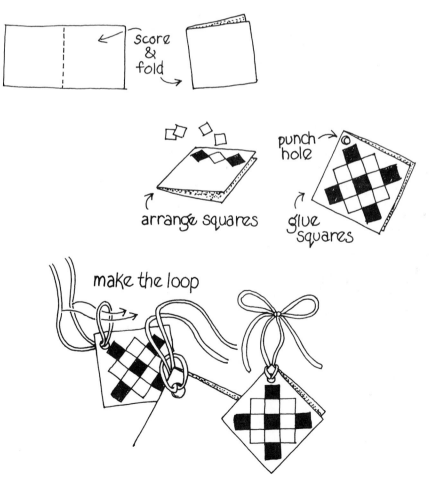

score & fold

arrange squares

punch hole

glue squares

make the loop

59

cutting line #1 ↴

cutting line #2 ↴

cutting line #3 ↴

cutting line #4 ↴

Woven Heart

1 Transfer the heart pattern to thin board or heavy paper to make the template as explained on page 15. Be sure to transfer all the cutting lines to the template.

2 Outline the template on the backing paper; cut out the heart and set aside.

If you are making more than one heart, outline and cut out all the backing pieces at one time.

3 Cut the template in two parts on cutting line #1 and discard the smaller part. For each heart, outline the remaining template piece once on each of the two different gift wraps. Cut on the outlines.

MATERIALS

Heavy paper or thin board for backing the heart (oaktag, Art Board, railroad board or 2-ply Bristol board)

Gift wrap in 2 different patterns (e.g., one country print and one contrasting geometric print): one piece of each, each piece about 3″ × 4″

Grosgrain ribbon, ⅜″ wide: one piece 9″ long for the bow; one piece 8″ long for the loop

Ruler, scissors

White glue

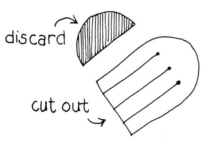

discard

cut out

draw template

outline

cut out

Draw cutting lines #2, #3 and #4 on the back of each piece of gift wrap and cut carefully on the cutting lines. Weave the two pieces of gift wrap together as shown below. When the two pieces are woven snugly, dab glue between the overlapping strips around the outer edge.

4 Bend the 8″ piece of ribbon in half and miter the ends steeply as shown. Glue the ends to the wrong side of the backing piece.

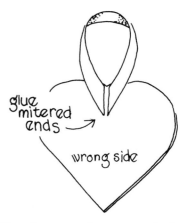

glue mitered ends →

wrong side

5 Glue the woven heart over the backing piece, wrong sides together, covering the ribbon ends. Use the 9″ piece of ribbon to make a pretty bow (see How to Tie a Bow, page 17); glue it in position on the center front of the woven heart, using a hair clip to hold the bow in place while the glue dries.

glue

Grapevine Wreath

Make your own natural wreath simply and inexpensively with wild grapevines—green, pliable and yours for the picking at the end of summer and in early autumn.

Gathering the vines: When you find a cache of the vines, pull them away from their hosts one at a time. Take a garden clippers with you to clip off each length of vine as you untangle it. It's nice if you can retain the curly tendrils, but often you must pull so hard to detach a vine that the tendrils break off. For each wreath collect an armful of vines, each 8-10 feet long; for a very large wreath you may need more.

Making the wreath: Strip all the leaves from the vines. Then take a handful of vines and hold them so the ends are staggered. Shape them into a circle of whatever diameter you like. Remember, the wreath can be large and sumptuous (perhaps $2\frac{1}{2}$ feet in diameter) or quite small and delicate (only 5"-6" in diameter).

stagger the ends ↗

shape vines into a circle

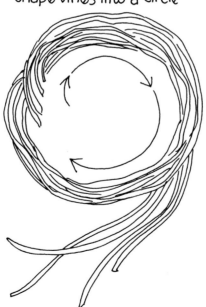

Keep winding in a circle until you have used up almost all of the vines. To end the wreath, wind the last two feet or so of each vine around the wreath and then tuck each end firmly between previously wound vines.

No string or wire is needed if you allow enough length for winding and tucking.

If you want more thickness, take two more vines, tuck the thicker ends into the wreath and wind them around and around the wreath as shown in the drawing. Repeat this until the wreath is the size you want.

Place the wreath flat in a warm, dry place until it dries and turns brown. When it is thoroughly dry and firm you can decorate and hang it.

wind vines around wreath; tuck ends between vines

finished wreath

Bandanna Bows
& Calico Stockings

Bread Dough
Birds

Wheat & Wildflower
Bouquets

Dragonflies

Yarn Girls &
Yarn Boys

4

Scrapbasket Ornaments

Scrapbasket Ornaments are made with odds and ends you have around the house—spools and cardboard, bits of rickrack and ribbon, leftover fabric and felt. Because the ornaments are so varied, the unifying element of my trees is color: the tree on page 66 is predominantly warm red, yellow and white and the tree on page 80 is cool blue, green and silver. Your scraps may be different colors so alter the color scheme accordingly.

Don't miss the Rickrack Basket, page 76, a perfect showpiece for a small table in the entryway of your house or apartment. It's ready to receive a stack of Christmas cards, a decorative arrangement of greens and Christmas balls or, as shown, a group of small gifts.

Gold Crocheted Stars

MATERIALS

**Metallic thread, one ball
(Since the thread I chose
was very thin, I wound it
into three equal balls and
crocheted with three strands
held as one. If you use another kind of yarn be sure to
use the appropriate crochet
hook. The instructions are
the same but the size of the
star will differ from the one
in the photograph)**

Crochet hooks E and 1

Blunt needle

White glue, paint brush

ABBREVIATIONS:

st = stitch

ch = chain stitch

sl st = slip stitch

sc = single crochet

hdc = half double crochet

dc = double crochet

tr = triple crochet

* = repeat directions
following

* as many times as indicated.

You will see this star on page 68 made with gold thread and on page 88 made with silver thread. If you're sharp you'll notice that they were made by a left-handed crocheter. Righties can hold a mirror up to the photograph to see how the stitches would look if made by a right-handed crocheter.

Round 1: Ch 10, join last st to 1st st with a sl st to form a ring.

Round 2: Ch 1, make 19 sc in ring. Join last st to 1st st with a sl st.

Round 3: Ch 1, 1 sc in each of next 3 sts. Ch 2 (this makes the bridge), * sc in each of next 4 sts, ch 2. Repeat from * 3 more times to complete the round. Join last st to 1st st with a sl st.

First point: Without cutting the thread, * Ch 6. Sl st back in 2nd ch from hook, sc in next ch, hdc in next ch, dc in next ch, tr in last ch. Skipping 2 sc of Round 2, sl st into next (4th) sc (the sc before the bridge). Make 2 sl sts in bridge. Sl st in next sc.

Repeat from * 4 more times to make the remaining four points of the star, ending with the 2 sl sts in the 5th bridge. End off.

The points of the star will probably be somewhat distorted when you finish crocheting them, so coax each one into shape. Steam iron the star lightly to set the shape.

Loop: Insert the #1 hook into the tip of one point and pull through a loop of a single thread. Ch 30 or enough chs to measure $4\frac{1}{2}''$. Sl st back into the tip. End off.

With the blunt needle, weave in all the loose ends of thread. Clip off any excess thread. Steam iron the star again to reset the shape if necessary.

Dilute a teaspoon or so of glue with a few drops of water. Brush diluted glue evenly over the back of the star to stiffen it and hold its shape. Place the star on waxed paper and let the glue dry thoroughly. You may then put another coat of glue on the back of the star if you prefer it even stiffer.

Christmas Flower

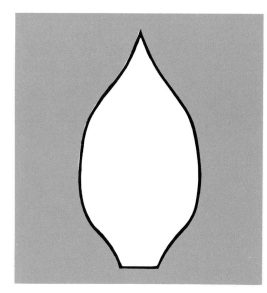

1 Transfer the pattern to heavy paper or thin board to make a template as described on page 15.

2 Pour out a little pile of seed beads. Smear glue on the top third of the Styrofoam ball and roll it around in the seed beads so some of the beads adhere to the ball. The beads will *not* cover the ball evenly. Set it aside to dry completely.

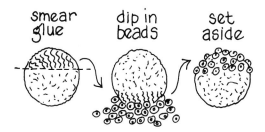

smear glue   dip in beads   set aside

3 Fold the red (or white) fabric in half lengthwise and iron on the fold. Slip the $2\frac{3}{4}'' \times 9\frac{1}{2}''$ piece of fusible web into the folded fabric, right up to the fold. Heat-baste the web in position by ironing along

the very edge of the fold. The cut edges of the fabric and web should be exactly even. If they are not, trim them just a fraction.

web

iron the fold

trim if necessary

Outline the template on the fabric six times, placing the stem end of the template even with the cut edges of the fabric and web.

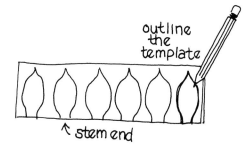

outline the template

↑ stem end

Slip one piece of wire under the top layer of fabric, centering it under the first petal outline, extending $\frac{3}{8}''$ at the lower edge. Repeat for the remaining five petals.

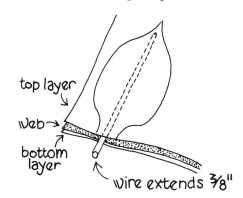

top layer

web →

bottom layer

wire extends $\frac{3}{8}''$

MATERIALS

Styrofoam ball, 1″ in diameter

Yellow seed beads

Light weight cotton or cotton-blend fabric: green, one piece $5\frac{1}{2}'' \times 3\frac{1}{2}''$ for the leaves; red or white, one piece $5\frac{1}{2}'' \times 9\frac{1}{2}''$ for the petals

Fusible web: one piece $2\frac{3}{4}'' \times 9\frac{1}{2}''$; one piece $2\frac{3}{4}'' \times 3\frac{1}{2}''$

20-gauge wire, 8 pieces, each $2\frac{1}{2}''$ long

Wirecutters

Grosgrain ribbon, $\frac{1}{8}''$ wide, one piece 8″ long for the loop

Heat-baste all the wires in place, moving the iron carefully so you don't disturb the position of the wires. Then fuse the fabric layers according to the manufacturer's instructions, ironing on the front *and* back.

Cut out all the petals on the outlines. Bend each wire as shown in the drawing.

4 Make two leaves the same way you made the petals, using the green fabric and the second piece of fusible web.

5 Put the parts together to make the flower. Squeeze out a little glue on some waxed paper. Dip the wire of one petal in the glue and insert the wire into the Styrofoam ball at the equator line. Dip the wire of a second petal in glue and insert it at the equator line opposite the first petal.

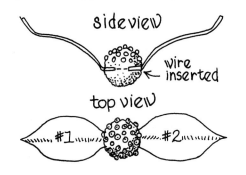

Dip in glue and insert the wires of petals #3 and #4 between petals #1 and #2 as shown. Dip in glue and insert the wires of petals #5 and #6 opposite petals #3 and #4.

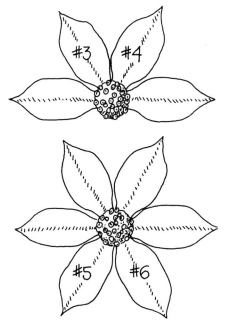

Then dip in glue and insert the wire of each green leaf between and immediately under any pair of petals.

6 To make the loop, fold the ribbon in half, dab glue on the ends and press the ends in position on the back of a petal.

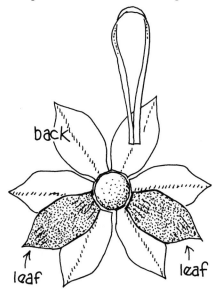

Spool Lantern

1 If the labels on the top and bottom of the spool are loose, peel them off. Smear glue all over the body of the spool (not on the ends). Spiral-wind the yellow cord snugly around the spool, beginning and ending on the same side. Trim off any excess cord. Let the glue dry.

2 Outline the round end of the spool twice on the colored board. Cut out the circles and punch a hole in the center of each. Glue one circle to each end of the spool.

3 Fold the ribbon in half and trim the ends on the diagonal. Make a knot about 2¾″ from the fold. Thread a bead onto the ribbon ends below the knot. Slip the ends of the ribbon through the center hole of the spool. NOTE: A pin or a needle will help you coax the ends of the ribbon out of the hole.

Thread the ends of the ribbon through another bead and knot them right below the bead.

MATERIALS

Empty spool (Use a spool that held 590 ft. of thread)

Yellow round cord, one piece 5 ft. long

Small piece of thin board like Art Board, poster board, or oaktag (Pick a color that contrasts with the yellow cord)

Hole puncher

Grosgrain ribbon, ⅛″ wide, one piece 20″ long for the loop

2 plastic beads with large holes

White glue

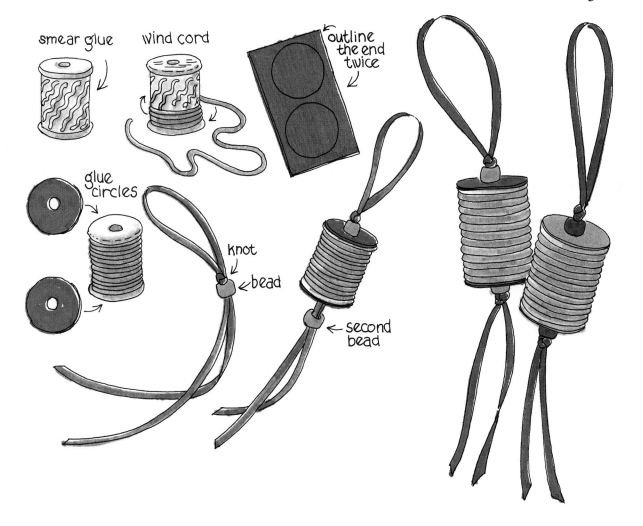

smear glue

wind cord

outline the end twice

glue circles

knot

bead

second bead

Rickrack Santa

MATERIALS

Heavy white paper (2-ply Bristol board, Art Board, card stock, etc.), if you are making more than one Santa

Cotton or cotton-blend fabric: one piece 5½″ × 9″ for the body; one piece 5″ × 3″ for the hat

Spray adhesive

Styrofoam ball, 1¼″-1⅜″ in diameter

Scraps of trims, as follows:

For the face: brush fringe, 1″ wide, one piece 5½″ long; 2 red beads; 2 blue beads; 4 straight pins

For the hat: one chenille stem (a longer, plushier version of a pipe cleaner), 1 small pompon

For the body: grosgrain ribbon, ⅜″ wide, one piece 3″ long; baby rickrack, one piece about 3″ long; medium rickrack, one piece about 12″ long

Grosgrain ribbon, ⅛″ wide, one piece 6″ long for the loop

White glue

1 Transfer the patterns to heavy paper or thin cardboard, following the instructions on page 15.

If you are making only one Santa, use the transferred hat pattern as a template (step 4) and use the transferred body pattern as the body (step 2).

If you are making more than one Santa, use the transferred patterns as templates. Reserve the hat template for use in step 4; outline the body template once on heavy white paper for each Santa, cut out each body on the outline and hold for use in step 2.

2 Make the body: Spray the heavy paper body with adhesive and center it on the wrong side of the 5½″ × 9″ piece of fabric. Turn over and smooth the fabric firmly over the heavy paper. Cut away most of the excess fabric, leaving ½″ allowance around the outer curve and at one end.

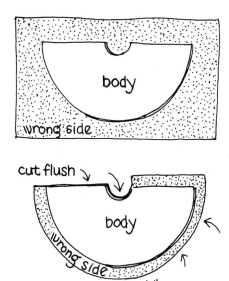

Shape the body into a cone, gluing the end with the extra fabric over the other end—make the heavy paper overlap ½″ at the top of the cone and 2″ at the bottom. The extra fabric will extend even further. Keep the overlaps even at the lower edge and trim them even at the top.

Apply glue sparingly to the wrong side of the extra fabric at the lower edge and turn under. Let the glue dry.

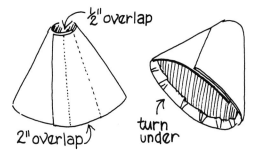

3 To attach the head: Press the Styrofoam ball firmly over the narrow end of the body, centered, to make an indentation in the ball. Remove the ball and squeeze glue into the indentation. Replace the ball, matching the indentation to the body. Holding the head securely in place, turn the body over and add a little glue inside the Santa, where the body and the head meet. Use a toothpick to apply the glue to the joint.

Turn the body right side up and set it aside while the glue dries.

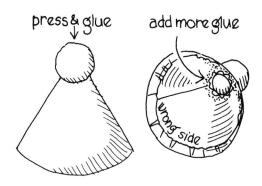

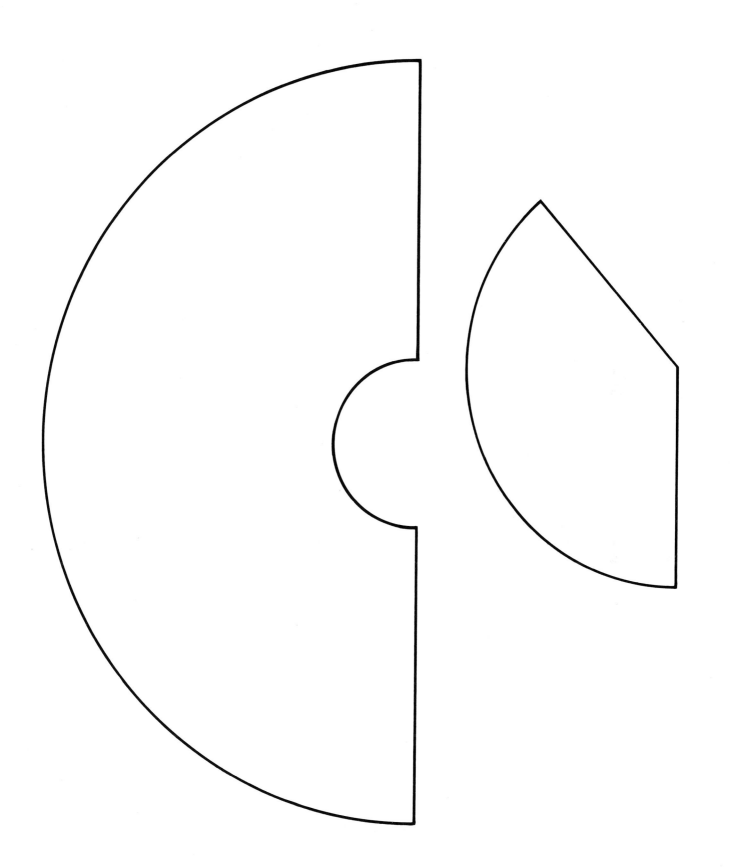

4 Make the hat: Outline the hat template on the wrong side of the 5″ × 3″ piece of fabric and cut it out on the outline. Shape the fabric into a cone with a point at the top, overlapping the bottom edges about $\frac{3}{8}$″. Glue the overlap and allow it to dry.

Fold the grosgrain ribbon in half and stitch the ends to the center back of the hat to make the loop.

Glue the small pompon over the point of the hat.

5 Decorate the body with the trims listed in *Materials,* following the drawing for guidance. Glue the $\frac{3}{8}$″ wide ribbon down the center front of the body. Glue the 3″ piece of baby rickrack over the ribbon. Glue the medium rickrack around the lower edge, beginning and ending at center back. Let the glue dry.

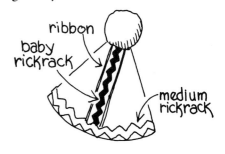

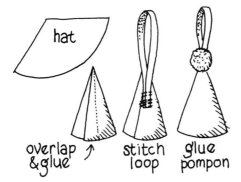

hat

overlap & glue ↑   stitch loop   glue pompon

ribbon
baby rickrack
medium rickrack

6 Add the facial features and the hat, using the trims listed in *Materials,* following the drawing for guidance. Apply glue to the heading of the brush fringe and wrap the fringe around the head as shown to form the beard and hair. Overlap the ends slightly at the center back and clip off the excess fringe. Reserve the excess for the moustache.

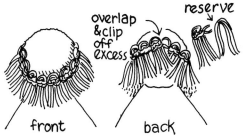

To make the eyes, anchor the two blue beads in the Styrofoam with straight pins.

To make the nose and mouth, anchor the two red beads about $\frac{1}{16}''$ apart, inserting the straight pins and beads only halfway.

To make the moustache, start with a small clump of threads pulled from the fringe that you reserved. Smear a little glue around the middle of the clump to hold the threads together. Center the moustache against the Styrofoam between the nose and mouth with a little dab of glue. Push the straight pins all the way into the Styrofoam—the moustache will be secured. Trim the moustache if desired.

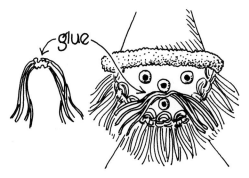

Apply glue sparingly to the wrong side of the lower edge of the hat and place the hat on the head, fitting it down snugly.

To make the "fur" edge of Santa's hat, shape a $6\frac{1}{4}''$ piece of chenille stem into a ring. Slip the ring over the hat, down to the lower edge, to check the fit. Cut off any excess. Remove the ring, apply glue to the lower edge of the hat and replace the ring, pressing it over the glue. The ends of the ring should meet at the center back of the hat. Be sure to keep the ribbon loop free.

Rickrack Basket

MATERIALS

Mushroom basket

High-gloss polyurethane

Brush, turpentine

One package of baby rick-rack; 2 packages of medium rickrack (Color A and Color B); One package of jumbo rickrack (Choose contrasting colors, following the photograph for ideas or inventing your own color scheme)

Grosgrain ribbon, $\frac{5}{8}''$ wide, one piece 22" long

White glue

Mushrooms often come to a store packed in thin wood baskets which are thrown out when empty. Ask the manager of your supermarket or produce store if you can take a few. Pick out the neatest, cleanest one for this project.

1 Give the basket two coats of polyurethane, allowing each coat to dry thoroughly. Clean the brush in turpentine and then with soap and water.

2 Iron all the rickrack to get out the packaging creases. Glue jumbo rickrack around the top and bottom bands, beginning and ending neatly at the center back, overlapping the ends about 1". Trim off any excess rickrack. Glue baby rickrack centered over the jumbo.

3 Cut off and glue a piece of the grosgrain ribbon vertically at the center front of the basket, cutting it to fit between the bands. Set aside the remaining ribbon. Now cut and glue pieces of the two colors of medium rickrack to fit vertically. Begin with Color A: first glue a piece on each side of the ribbon, cutting each piece to fit; then glue pieces of Color A all around the basket, leaving about $1\frac{5}{8}''$ between them. Glue pieces of Color B, cut to fit, between the pieces of Color A.

4 Make a pretty bow with the remaining ribbon (see How to Tie a Bow on page 17) and glue the bow to the center front of the basket. Clip the bow in position with a clothespin while the glue dries.

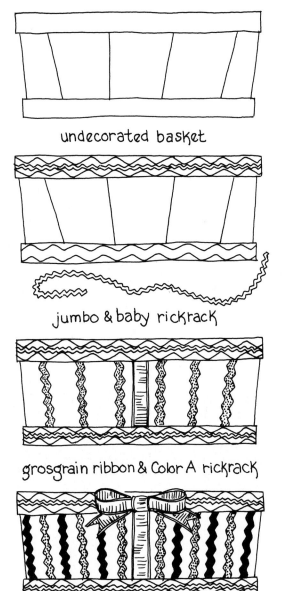

undecorated basket

jumbo & baby rickrack

grosgrain ribbon & Color A rickrack

Color B rickrack & grosgrain bow

*Scrapwraps (page 78), Rickrack Basket
(page 76)*

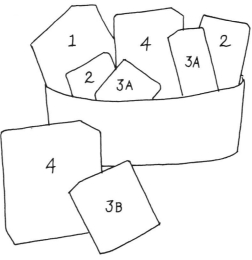

77

Scrapwraps

MATERIALS

Solid color gift wrap

Scraps of yarn, rickrack and ball fringe

Transparent tape

White glue

Here are five gift wrap designs that make use of trims left over from sewing or craft projects. If your selection of leftovers happens to be different from mine, just use mine as a starting point and dream up a whole new set of your own scrapwraps.

Start by wrapping the packages in solid color gift wrap paper, which will set off the trims to advantage. Also, it's a good idea to iron the rickrack (or any other trim) if it is creased.

Scrapwrap #1: Cut two pieces of medium rickrack, each long enough to wrap once around the package and overlap about 1″ on the back. Wrap them around and tape the ends on the back of the package. Cut two more pieces, each long enough to wrap around the package in the other direction. Wrap these around and tape the ends on the back.

Scrapwrap #2: Using two strands of yarn, tie the package as if you were tying with ribbon. Knot the yarn on the top of the package. Do not clip off the excess yarn. Cut ten pieces of yarn and tie them to the top, using the yarn ends as shown in the drawing. Give the yarn ends a haircut to even them up. Cut one pompon (or more if the package and yarn tie are large) from ball fringe and glue it over the knot.

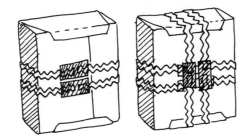

Scrapwrap #3A: Cut two pieces of baby rickrack, each long enough to wrap around the package and overlap ½″ on the back. Keeping the pieces parallel, about ½″ apart, wrap them around and tape the ends on the back of the package. Cut two more pieces, each long enough to wrap around the package in the other direction, wrap these around and tape the ends on the back. Cut a pompon from ball fringe and glue it to the package over the intersection.

Scrapwrap #3B: Tape the rickrack to the package as described above. Cut nine pompons from ball fringe and glue them to the package at the intersection as shown in the photograph.

Scrapwrap #4: Using four very long strands of yarn, tie the package as if you were tying with ribbon, making a bow on top. Now tie another bow and then another (third) bow, without cutting the yarn. Fan the bows out and cut off the excess yarn ends. You will have a mound of yarn in the middle. Cut six pompons from ball fringe, glue one on the center of the mound and five surrounding it.

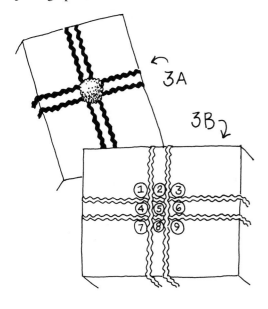

Snapshot with Rickrack Frame

For this ornament, select a snapshot with a strong central image—a family group, two or three children sitting close together, a close-up of your pet. Stay away from shots of scenery or shots in which the people are tiny.

1 With the compass draw a 3″ diameter circle on the heavy paper; this will be your template for cutting out the snapshot. Using the compass again, draw a 3½″ diameter circle on the cardboard; this will be the backing piece. Cut out both circles.

2 Outline the 3″ circle on the snapshot, centering the most important part of the picture. Cut out the snapshot on the outline.

3 Prepare the backing: Smear glue sparingly on one side of the cardboard circle. Center the piece of fabric on the circle

(right side up, wrong side on the glue) and smooth it out. Turn the fabric and cardboard over and cut away most of the excess fabric, leaving only about ½″ of fabric all around the cardboard. Snip the fabric as shown. Apply glue to the edges of the cardboard and smooth the ½″ allowance up and over the glue. Let the glue dry.

smooth fabric over cardboard

right side

cut out

wrong side

snip

glue

smooth up & over glue

MATERIALS

Shirt cardboard (or equivalent), one piece 4″ square

Heavy paper, one piece about 3½″ square, or a 3″ × 5″ index card

Compass

Snapshot, at least 3″ square

Cotton or cotton-blend fabric, one piece 5″ square
Silver (or other color) middy braid, ¼″ wide; one piece 5″ long for the loop; one piece 12″ long for the bow

Medium rickrack, 2 pieces, each 13″ long, in contrasting colors

White glue

4 Smear glue on the back of the snapshot and center it on the exposed cardboard of the backing piece. Place a couple of heavy books on the snapshot to keep it flat while the glue dries.

When the glue is dry, fold the 5″ piece of middy braid as shown and glue the ends to the backing piece, just above the snapshot, to make a loop. Be sure the loop is at the top of the snapshot!

5 Interlock the two contrasting pieces of rickrack to make one piece about 12″-13″ long. Iron the piece flat. Apply glue to the edge of the snapshot and to the fabric around the snapshot. Position the rickrack on the glue, beginning and ending at the bottom of the snapshot. Let the ends of the rickrack overlap about ¼″; trim off any ex-

cess. Clip the overlapping ends of the rickrack to the backing piece with a clothespin while the glue dries.

6 Tie the remaining piece of middy braid in a bow (see How to Tie a Bow, page 17). Attach the bow to the rickrack just below the loop by applying glue to the back of the bow loops, the center knot and part of the braid as shown. Press the bow in position, clipping with clothespins while the glue dries if necessary.

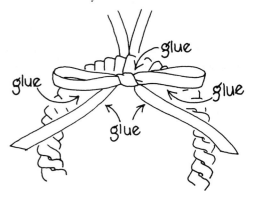

Christmas Ball with Glitter Trees

Before you begin, prepare a place where you can hang the balls at each stage while the glitter dots dry. One possibility is to cut several 8″ pieces of thin, sturdy wire, bend each one and tape it to a table edge as shown below. Another even simpler arrangement is to wind pieces of masking tape around a wire hanger and hook the balls over the wire between the pieces of tape.

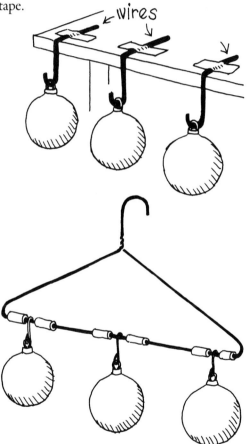

1 Apply the vertical dots that divide the ball in quarters: Start with Color A, with the top of the ball facing you. Squeeze the glitter pen to make dots on the ball at 12, 3, 6 and 9 o'clock. Add a few more dots in each direction. Then turn the ball to one side and work down, applying the dots in as straight a line as you can. Repeat this for each side. Let the dots dry.

Now turn the ball so the bottom faces you. Continue making dots all the way to the center bottom. Let the dots dry.

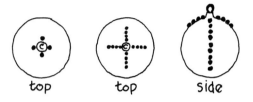

2 Make the trees using the color drawing above as a guide. Each tree is positioned between two vertical rows of dots. Using Color B, center the first dot of the tree about one third of the way down the ball. Below the first dot make a pyramid of dots, ending with a row of five dots. Turn the ball to the opposite side and repeat. Let the dots dry.

When all the dots are dry, make the trees on the two remaining sides. Let those dots dry, too.

With Color C add one dot to the top of each tree. With Color A add two dots to the bottom of each tree to make the trunk. Let the dots dry.

3 Thread the grosgrain ribbon through the wire loop at the top of the ball. Tie a bow and trim the ribbon ends on the diagonal. Hang the ball on the tree with an ordinary ornament hook.

MATERIALS

Christmas ball, about 2¼″ in diameter

Glitter pens in 3 colors: Color A for the vertical dots and tree trunk; Color B for the tree; Color C for the dot at the top of the tree (A glitter pen is a pointy-tipped tube in which glitter and glue are combined; squeeze the tube and the glitter comes out either in a thin line or in dots. Practice making a few rows of dots on paper before you begin this project. If the pen clogs, use a toothpick or a large needle to clear the tip)

Grosgrain ribbon, ⅜″ wide, one piece 14″ long for the bow

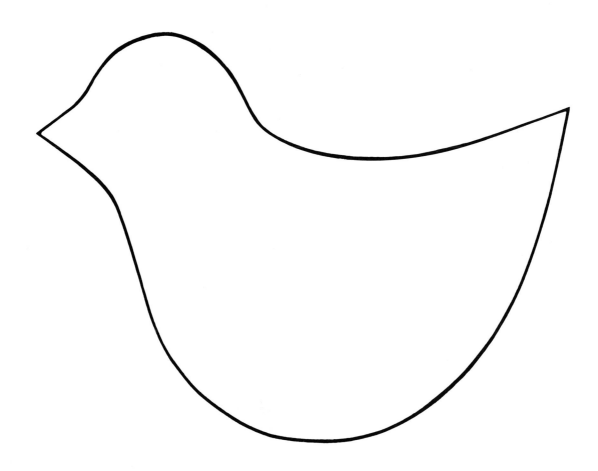

Bluebird with Eyelet Wings

1 Transfer the patterns to heavy paper or thin board to make a template, following the instructions on page 15.

2 Outline the template, centered, on the wrong side of one piece of fabric. Pin the two pieces of fabric with right sides together. Fold the grosgrain ribbon in half and insert the ends between the two pieces of fabric as shown below, sliding the ends up so they extend $\frac{1}{2}''$ above the outline. Pin the ribbon in place.

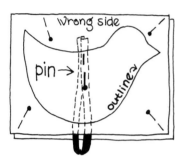

When the bird is stitched, the ribbon ends will be caught in the stitching. When the bird is then turned right side out, presto! you have an attached loop.

3 Straight-stitch around the outline, leaving a 2″ opening at the bottom of the bird where the ribbon emerges. Cut away the excess fabric close to the stitching, except around the opening.

4 Turn the bird right side out and iron it. Turn under and iron the seam allowances at the opening. Stuff the bird with polyester and then hand stitch the opening closed.

5 Fold and iron each piece of eyelet as shown. Hand stitch each piece to one side of the bird to make the wings, checking the photograph for placement.

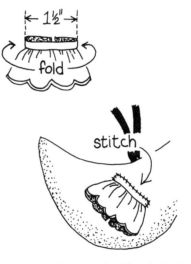

Glue one sequin to each side of the head to make the eyes.

MATERIALS

Cotton or cotton-blend print fabric, 2 pieces, each 5″ × 7″

Grosgrain ribbon, $\frac{1}{8}''$ wide, one piece 7″ long for the loop

Polyester stuffing

Ruffled eyelet, 1″ wide: 2 pieces, each 3″ long

2 sequins for the eyes

White glue

Felt Tree

Felt, 4 pieces, each 6″ square

Polyester batting, 2 pieces, each 6 ″ square

Cord or ribbon, $\frac{1}{8}$″ wide, one piece 7″ long for the loop

Medium sequins (8 mm)

Grosgrain ribbon, $\frac{3}{8}$″ wide, one piece 12″ long for the bow

1 Transfer the pattern to heavy paper or thin board to make a template as explained on page 15.

2 Outline the template on one piece of felt. Make a sandwich with the outlined felt on top, one piece of batting in the middle and another piece of felt on the bottom. Pin the layers together within the outline.

Repeat this process with the remaining felt and batting.

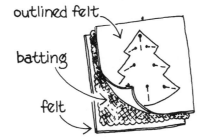

outlined felt

batting

felt

3 Fold the $\frac{1}{8}$″ wide cord (or ribbon) in half and insert the ends between the felt and batting of one sandwich, extending 1″ down at the point of the tree. Pin the ends in position. When you stitch the outline, the ends will be caught securely to make the loop.

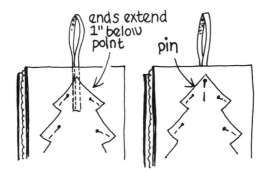

ends extend 1″ below point

pin

4 Using a tight zigzag, stitch all the way around the outline of each tree. Carefully cut away the excess felt and batting just outside the zigzag stitching. Be sure to cut *around* the cord—don't accidentally cut the loop off!

5 Place the two trees together, matching the edges. Straight-stitch down the center, through all layers. Iron open the sections.

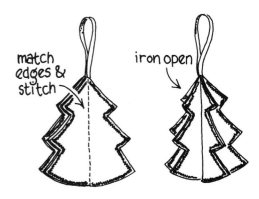

match edges & stitch

iron open

6 Put the tree down flat, with two sections (one side) showing. Use a toothpick to dab one section randomly with seven or eight dots of glue. Place a sequin on each dot. Repeat for the other section. Let this side dry completely, then turn the tree over to expose a fresh side.

Repeat for all sides.

7 Tie the grosgrain ribbon in a pretty bow (see How to Tie a Bow, page 17). With a few stitches, tack the bow to the cord just above the point of the tree.

sequins in place

dots of glue

Silver Crocheted Star

MATERIALS

**Metallic thread, one ball
(Since the thread I chose
was very thin, I wound it
into three equal balls and
crocheted with three strands
held as one. If you use another kind of yarn be sure to
use the appropriate crochet
hook. The instructions are
the same but the size of the
star will differ from the one
in the photograph)**

Crochet hooks E and 1

Blunt needle

White glue, paint brush

ABBREVIATIONS:

st = stitch

ch = chain stitch

sl st = slip stitch

sc = single crochet

hdc = half double crochet

dc = double crochet

tr = triple crochet

* = repeat directions
following

* as many times as indicated.

You will see this star on page 68 made with gold thread and on page 88 made with silver thread. If you're sharp you'll notice that they were made by a left-handed crocheter. Righties can hold a mirror up to the photograph to see how the stitches would look if made by a right-handed crocheter.

Round 1: Ch 10, join last st to 1st st with a sl st to form a ring.

Round 2: Ch 1, make 19 sc in ring. Join last st to 1st st with a sl st.

Round 3: Ch 1, 1 sc in each of next 3 sts. Ch 2 (this makes the bridge), * sc in each of next 4 sts, ch 2. Repeat from * 3 more times to complete the round. Join last st to 1st st with a sl st.

First point: Without cutting the thread, * Ch 6. Sl st back in 2nd ch from hook, sc in next ch, hdc in next ch, dc in next ch, tr in last ch. Skipping 2 sc of Round 2, sl st into next (4th) sc (the sc before the bridge). Make 2 sl sts in bridge. Sl st in next sc.
   Repeat from * 4 more times to make the remaining four points of the star, ending with the 2 sl sts in the 5th bridge. End off.
   The points of the star will probably be somewhat distorted when you finish crocheting them, so coax each one into shape. Steam iron the star lightly to set the shape.

Loop: Insert the #1 hook into the tip of one point and pull through a loop of a single thread. Ch 30 or enough chs to measure $4\frac{1}{2}''$. Sl st back into the tip. End off.

With the blunt needle, weave in all the loose ends of thread. Clip off any excess thread. Steam iron the star again to reset the shape if necessary.
   Dilute a teaspoon or so of glue with a few drops of water. Brush diluted glue evenly over the back of the star to stiffen it and hold its shape. Place the star on waxed paper and let the glue dry thoroughly. You may then put another coat of glue on the back of the star if you prefer it even stiffer.

Holiday Table Decorations

A beautiful meal deserves a beautiful table, especially at holiday time. Use the ornaments from this chapter to create festive centerpieces and place settings, as suggested in the drawings below.

5

Children's Ornaments

These miniature toys, animals and dolls for the tree remind us that Christmas can be a world of wonder for a child. A children's tree should look very abundant so string plenty of multi-colored lights and paper chains, hang all the ornaments you can make and clip on some Bandanna Bows. Fill in generously with candy canes and add red balls if necessary.

If your kids love teddy bears, stitch up the Teddy Bear Tree Skirt (page 109) or the Teddy Bear Stockings (page 115) to match the teddies on the tree. And for a really special once-a-year treat, make a Cookie Tree (page 119) for the kids' room.

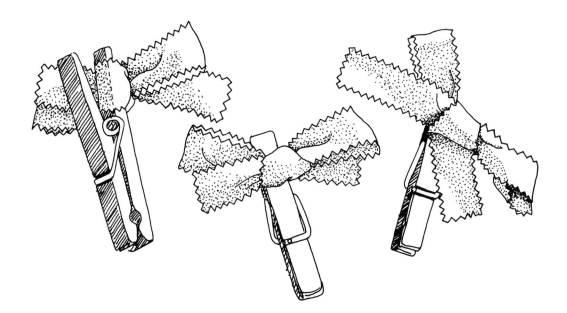

Bandanna Bows

Fold the fabric in half and iron the fold. Slip the fusible web into the folded fabric right up to the fold. Iron the fabric and web together according to the manufacturer's instructions.

Mark 1″-wide strips on the fabric; you will have 35 or 36 strips marked. Use the pinking shears first to cut the strips apart and then to cut off a bit of each end of each strip.

Glue each strip to a clothespin as shown in the drawing and let the glue dry thoroughly. Tie the strip in a bow around the clothespin. NOTE: The strip will be rather stiff and hard to tie, but this will give you a very crisp, pretty bow.

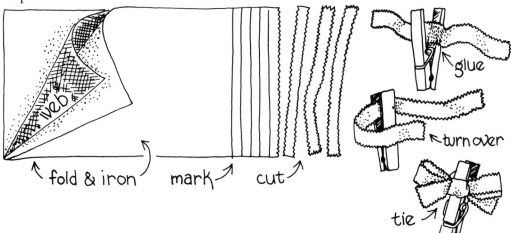

fold & iron   mark   cut   glue   turn over   tie

Stuffed Teddy Bear

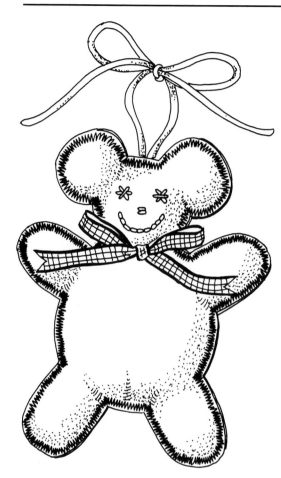

Fasten the embroidered piece of felt over the second piece of felt with pins at the tummy, arms, legs and ears.

3 Using a tight zigzag, stitch over the outline leaving an unstitched opening on the side of the bear as shown. Carefully cut off the excess felt just outside the zigzag stitching *except* around the unstitched section.

Stuff the bear sparingly with polyester stuffing. Pin the opening closed and finish stitching on the outline. Cut away the excess felt.

MATERIALS
2 pieces of felt, each 5″ × 7″
Embroidery thread
Taffeta ribbon, ⅜″ wide, one piece 12″ long
Polyester stuffing
Yarn for the loop

1 Transfer the pattern (page 94) to thin cardboard or heavy paper to make a template, as explained on page 15.

2 Outline the template on one piece of felt. Embroider the eyes, nose and mouth as shown in the drawing, using two strands of embroidery thread doubled over to make four strands.

Hand stitch the center of the ribbon to the neck of the bear but do not tie the bow yet.

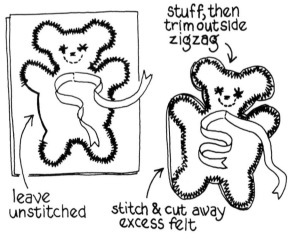

stuff, then trim outside zigzag

leave unstitched

stitch & cut away excess felt

4 Tie the ribbon in a bow and trim the ends neatly. Cut a 16″ piece of yarn, fold it in half and tack the fold to the back of the bear at the zigzag stitching between the ears. Tie the ends of yarn to the tree in a bow.

94

Little House

Use contrasting colors for the different parts of the house. For example, if the house is yellow, the door might be red, the windows green or blue, the roof a red print and the loop braid trim might be green. If the house is red, you can make the door white, the windows yellow, the roof a print with a white background and the loop braid trim might pick up a color in the roof.

1 Draw light pencil lines on the thin board square as shown in the drawing. Cut on the dotted lines and score lightly with the mat knife on the heavy lines. Fold the board and cut a notch in the roof as shown.

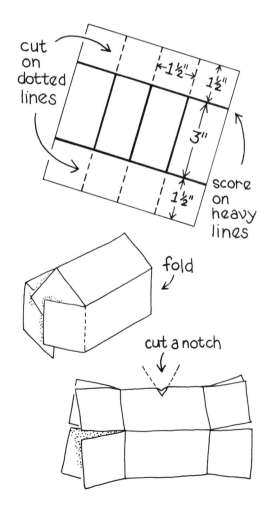

2 Add two windows and a door to each side of the house. For each door, glue two 1″-long pieces of ribbon in the center of each side. For each window, glue a ½″-long piece of ribbon to the left or right of a door.

3 Glue together the top two squares of one side as shown, clipping the squares with clothespins while the glue dries. Repeat this process for the second side. Then overlap and glue the lower squares on one side, clipping again to hold them while the glue dries. Repeat for the second side.

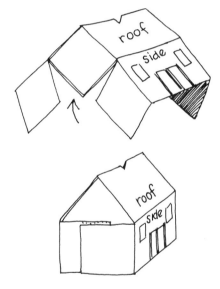

4 Cut a piece of calico (or other print fabric) just a jot larger than 3″ × 3″. Iron it in half, then fold it in quarters and cut a little notch at the point as shown. Apply glue to

MATERIALS

Thin board (Art Board, oak-tag, railroad board or 2-ply Bristol board), one piece 6″ × 6″ for the house

Mat knife

Scraps of grosgrain ribbon, 1″ wide, to contrast with the thin board

Scrap of calico or other print fabric

Loop braid in a color to contrast with the fabric

Cord, soutache or middy braid, one piece 10″ long for the loop

White glue

the roof of the house and smooth the fabric over the glue, matching the ironed fold to the point of the roof. Cut two pieces of loop braid, each exactly the width of the roof. Apply glue to the back of each piece and place one in position on each side at the edge of the roof.

5 Knot together the ends of the cord (or soutache or middy braid). Slip the unknotted end into the house and through the hole in the roof. Hang the house on the tree by this loop.

3"+

fold
in half

fold in quarters,
cut a notch

smooth over glue

loop braid

The Sockdoll Family

MATERIALS FOR MAKING THE WHOLE FAMILY

One pair of solid color baby socks, size 5-5½

One small child's mitten

Polyester stuffing

Assorted colors of small beads for the facial features

Red thread

Ribbon, ⅛″ wide: 3 pieces, each 6″ long, for the loops

White glue

MATERIALS FOR THE MOTHER

Embroidered ribbon, ½″ wide, one piece 10″ long for the scarf

2 small buttons

2 medium pompons

MATERIALS FOR THE FATHER

Grosgrain ribbon, ⅜″ wide, one piece 10″ long for the scarf

2 small buttons

One large pompon

MATERIALS NEEDED FOR THE BABY

Taffeta ribbon, ⅜″ wide, one piece 7″ long for the scarf

One small pompon

Cut the baby socks into four parts as shown and discard one ankle section. Cut the mitten into three sections as shown and discard the leftover piece.

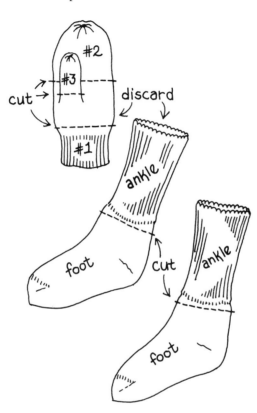

MAMA SOCKDOLL

1 Make the body and head: With polyester stuffing, stuff the foot section of one sock to the line indicated in the drawing below. Don't stuff it too much—just make it plump and soft.

Turn under the raw edge and close the opening. Make a line of running stitch around the turned-under edge, pull the thread to gather the sock tightly, secure the thread. Then take a few stitches back and forth across the gathering. This will be the back of the sock doll.

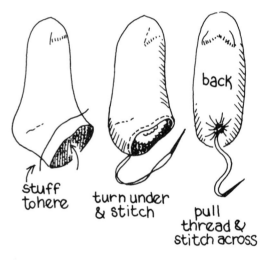

Tie off the neckline about 2″ from the toe to form the head. Wind a double thread tightly around the neckline several times and tie the thread securely. Clip off the excess thread.

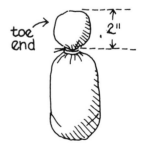

98

2 Make and attach the mother's hat: Turn mitten section #1 wrong side out and make a line of straight stitch ½″ from the raw edge. Pull the thread to gather tightly and then secure the thread.

Turn the hat right side out. Steam iron the gathers gently to set them and flatten them a bit. Put the hat on the mother and, with needle and thread, tack it in place all around the edge. Glue two medium pompons to the top of the hat.

PAPA SOCKDOLL

1 Repeat step 1 of Mama Sockdoll.

2 Make and attach the father's hat: Turn under the raw edge of mitten section #2 and iron it on the fold. Put the cap on Papa Sockdoll and tack it in place all around the ironed edge. Cut the large pompon flat on one side and glue the flat side to the top of the cap.

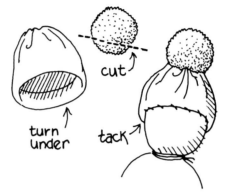
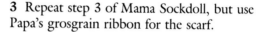

3 Repeat step 3 of Mama Sockdoll, but use Papa's grosgrain ribbon for the scarf.

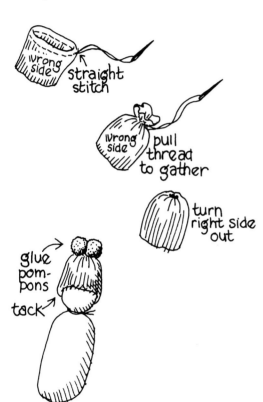

3 Put the finishing touches on the mother, following the color drawing for guidance. Sew on beads for the eyes and nose. Double a length of red thread and stitch a smiling mouth. Sew two buttons on the front, with the first button about ½″ below the neckline. Tie the embroidered ribbon scarf around the neck (off center as in the drawing), trim the ends and tack them to the body with dabs of white glue.

Fold a 6″ piece of ⅛″ wide ribbon in half and stitch the ends to the back of Mama's hat to make the loop.

BABY SOCKDOLL

1 Make the body and head: Turn the remaining piece of sock (the ankle section) inside out. Draw a curve on the sock as shown and stitch by hand or machine along the curve. Trim away the excess fabric close to the stitching to leave a curved edge. Turn the sock right side out. Stuff the sock plumply to make the body.

Close the open end. Make a line of running stitch around the edge and pull the thread to gather the sock tightly. Secure the thread.

Tie off the neckline, about 1″ from the top, to form the head. Wind a double thread tightly around the neckline several times and tie it securely. Clip off the excess thread.

2 Make and attach the baby's hat: Turn under the raw edge of mitten section #3 and iron the fold. Put this cap on the baby's head and tack it in place with needle and thread. Glue a small pompon to the top of the cap.

3 Put the finishing touches on the baby, following the color drawing for guidance. Sew beads in position for the eyes, nose and mouth. Tie the taffeta ribbon scarf around the neck, trim the ends and tack them to the body with dabs of glue. Fold a 6″ long piece of $\frac{1}{8}$″ wide ribbon in half and stitch the ends to the back of the baby's cap to make the loop.

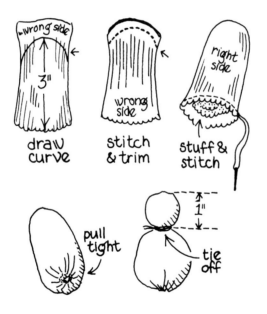

Caterpillar Clown

1 Prepare the pieces for the head, body and hat. Use a compass and ruler to outline the following:

- on white board, two circles, each $1\frac{1}{2}''$ in diameter, for the head
- on red board, two circles, each $2\frac{1}{2}''$ in diameter, for the body
- on red board, two triangles, as shown below, for the hat

2 For each leg cut two paper strips, each $11\frac{3}{4}'' \times \frac{3}{4}''$; for each arm, cut two paper strips, each $10'' \times \frac{3}{4}''$.

Fold each pair of strips to make caterpillars as shown in the drawing, gluing the ends together at top and bottom and trimming off any excess paper. Fold the top of each caterpillar on the diagonal to make tabs.

MATERIALS

Thin board such as Art Board, oaktag or railroad board, in red and white or any 2 contrasting colors

Compass, ruler

High-gloss gift wrap or other light weight paper for the arms and legs

5 medium pompons

2 small pompons

Satin ribbon, $\frac{1}{8}''$ wide: 2 pieces, each 7" long, for the bow tie and the loop (I used one piece of red and one piece of green but you may prefer to use only one contrasting color)

Sequins: 1 large (10 mm), 1 medium (8 mm) and 1 small (6 mm) for the face

White glue

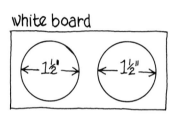

white board

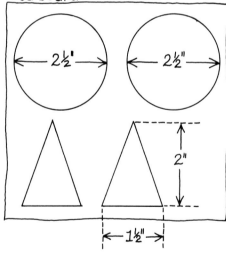

red board

glue · trim · fold up to make tab

Cut out all the pieces on the outlines. The clown is made up of a front and a back, with the arms and legs sandwiched between. That is the reason for cutting out two of each part. NOTE: If you are making more than one or two clowns, make templates for the circles and triangle and outline the templates on the thin board instead of repeatedly using the compass and ruler.

Set the pieces aside.

Toy Drum with Drumsticks (page 106),
Caterpillar Clown (page 101), Woodscrap
Horse (page 104)

3 Glue one head, one body, the arms, the legs and one hat together: First glue the head to the body as shown below. Next, glue the hat to the head, off center. Then dab glue on the tabs of the arms and legs and put them in place on the back of the body.

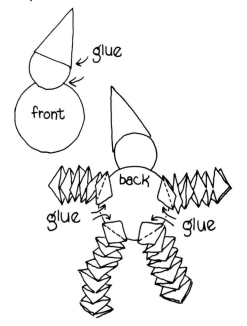

4 Fold one piece of ribbon in half and glue the ends to the back of the hat and head to make the loop. Be sure the ends of the ribbon are side by side as shown. Let the glue dry.

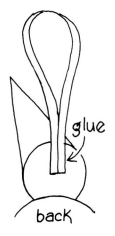

5 To finish the back of the clown, glue the second body over the clown's body, covering the four tabs. Glue the second head over the clown's head and the second hat over the clown's hat. All the edges should match.

6 Tie the remaining piece of ribbon into a small bow (see How to Tie a Bow, page 17) and glue it in place at the neck, following the photograph for guidance. Glue the two small pompons below the bow. Glue one medium pompon at the end of each arm and leg and one on the tip of the hat.
  Glue the small sequin to the face for a nose. Cut the large sequin into a smiling mouth and glue it below the nose. Cut the medium sequin in half and glue the halves to the face for eyes.

Woodscrap Horse

MATERIALS

Scraps of wood, cut with a dovetail saw: pine lattice, $1\frac{1}{4}'' \times \frac{1}{4}''$, 2 pieces, each $3\frac{1}{2}''$ long, for the body; pine lattice, $1\frac{3}{4}'' \times \frac{1}{4}''$, one piece cut as shown below for the head, one piece 1″ long for the neck and one piece $\frac{1}{2}''$ long for the tail

Dowel, $\frac{3}{8}''$ in diameter: 4 pieces, each $2\frac{1}{2}''$ long, for the legs. *Note:* Sand all the wood scraps and dowels smooth and brush off all sawdust.

Sandpaper, medium and fine

White acrylic paint, brush

Red glitter

High-gloss polyurethane

Brush, turpentine

Gold fringe, $\frac{1}{2}''$ wide, one short scrap

Grosgrain ribbon, $\frac{3}{8}''$ wide, one piece $4\frac{1}{4}''$ long

Satin ribbon, $\frac{1}{8}''$ wide, one piece 18″ long for the loop

Scrap of felt, 1″ × 2″

White glue

The drawing below shows the pieces of pine lattice and dowel that are specified in the materials list.

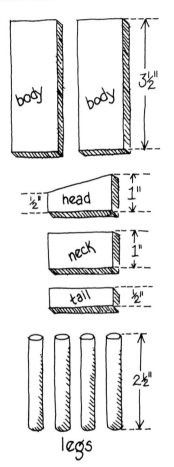

1 Sand a section of each dowel flat by placing the sandpaper on a flat surface and rubbing the dowel firmly back and forth over it, keeping the dowel very steady.

2 Glue the head to the neck as shown and let the glue dry. Glue the neck and tail between the body pieces. Let the glue dry. Glue the flat sanded sections of two legs to one side of the body. Let the glue dry.

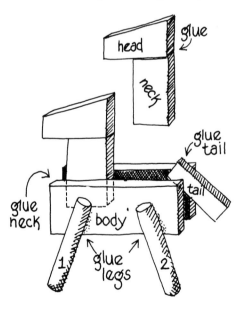

On the opposite side of the body, mark the position of the second pair of legs, matching the position of the previously glued pair. Glue the remaining dowels on the marks and let the glue dry.

3 Paint the entire horse with two coats of white acrylic, letting the paint dry thoroughly after each coat. Clean the brush with soap and water.

4 Smear glue on one foot. Dip the foot firmly in glitter to cover the glue. Tap off the excess glitter. Repeat this process for the other three feet. Let the glue dry.

5 Pour some polyurethane into a paper cup, dip one foot into the cup, lift and let the excess drip off. Repeat for the other three feet, then use the brush to paint the rest of the horse with polyurethane. Let the horse dry thoroughly on waxed paper. Clean the brush first in turpentine and then with soap and water.

6 Glue a short piece of gold fringe around the head to make a forelock. Glue two strips of fringe in place—one on each side of the neck—to make the mane. Glue another short piece of fringe around the tail.

Tip: Use hair clips or clothespins to hold the fringe in place while the glue dries.

Cut two little bits of $\frac{1}{8}''$ wide ribbon and glue them in place for the eyes. Glue the grosgrain ribbon around the middle of the horse, overlapping the ends at the top. Let the glue dry. Glue the satin ribbon over the grosgrain ribbon, centered, and tie a double knot.

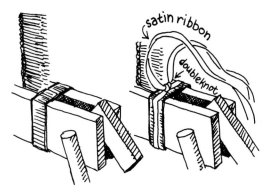

Fold the felt piece in half and cut a little notch in the center. Slip the ends of the satin ribbon through the hole and push the felt down so the knot comes through the hole. Apply glue to the underside of the felt and press the felt into place to make a saddle.

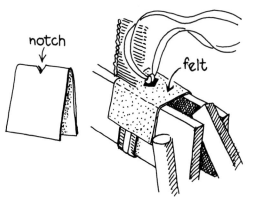

Tie the horse to the tree with the ends of the satin ribbon.

Toy Drum with Drumsticks

MATERIALS

Cardboard tube from a roll of paper towels, approximately $1\frac{3}{4}''$ in diameter

Mat knife with sharp new blade

Scraps of the following fabrics:

Thin cotton or cotton-blend in a solid color for the top and bottom of the drum

White or light colored felt

Cotton or cotton-blend print for the side of the drum

Grosgrain ribbon, $\frac{1}{8}''$ wide: one piece 8" long for the loop; 10 pieces, each $1\frac{3}{4}''$ long, for the side decorations

Grosgrain ribbon, $\frac{3}{8}''$ wide: 2 pieces, each 8" long

10 medium (8 mm) sequins

Dowel, $\frac{3}{16}''$ in diameter: 2 pieces, each $3\frac{1}{2}''$ long

2 medium pompons

White glue

1 With the mat knife cut off a 2" section of the cardboard tube.

2 Cut two circles of solid color fabric, each with a diameter 1" wider than the diameter of the tube. Smear glue around one end of the tube as shown below. Center a circle of fabric over the end and press the edges of the fabric down onto the glue, stretching the fabric taut.

Repeat on the other end of the tube. Let the glue dry, then clip off the excess folds of fabric.

3 Cut a strip of felt $6\frac{1}{2}'' \times 1\frac{7}{8}''$. Glue the felt around the tube, clipping off any excess to make a perfectly smooth joint with no overlap. Cut a strip of print fabric $7'' \times 2''$. Glue this over the felt, overlapping the ends of the print fabric about $\frac{1}{2}''$. The overlap will be the back of the drum.

4 Fold the 8" piece of $\frac{1}{8}''$ wide grosgrain ribbon in half and glue the ends to the back of the drum to make the loop.

5 Glue one piece of $\frac{3}{8}''$ wide grosgrain ribbon around the drum, even with the top edge, overlapping the ends $\frac{1}{2}''$ at the back. Clip off any excess ribbon. Repeat with the second piece of ribbon at the bottom edge of the drum. Let the glue dry.

Starting at the front, glue the 10 pieces of $\frac{1}{8}''$ wide grosgrain ribbon around the drum. *Tip:* Hold each little piece of ribbon in a tweezers and apply glue to the back with a toothpick. Place the pieces on the diagonal, overlapping the ends of ribbon to make points about $1\frac{1}{4}''$ apart.

Glue a sequin over each point.

6 Glue a pompon over one end of each piece of dowel to make the drumsticks. Glue one drumstick flat across the top of the drum. Rest the second drumstick across the first drumstick and the edge of the drum as shown in the photograph on page 102. Glue it in place at the points of contact. Don't move the drum until the glue dries thoroughly.

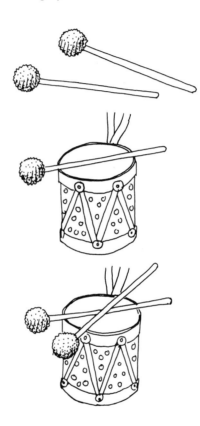

3/8" wide
ribbon

1/8" wide
ribbon

sequins

Teddy Bear Tree Skirt (page 109)

Teddy Bear Tree Skirt

1 Transfer and make a template from the large bear pattern shown on page 111, following the instructions on page 15. Set the template aside for now.

2 Prepare the circle of felt by ironing it well and cutting a hole 6″ in diameter in the center.

3 Cut the shearling into strips 4″ wide. You will need enough strips to make a length of 155″–156″, approximately the circumference of the circle. Follow one of the cutting diagrams below, which allows you some extra fabric.

If the edge of the fabric is messy or soiled you may want to start cutting your first strip an inch or two from the edge. The extra fabric allows you to do so.

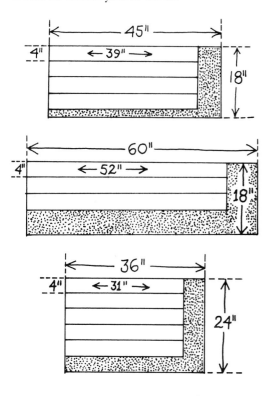

Tip: When cutting shearling, slide the points of the scissors very close to the backing fabric. By doing this, you avoid cutting through the actual fur pile, resulting in much tidier edges and less shedding of little puffets of fur.

4 Fold each strip of shearling *almost* in half lengthwise, wrong sides together, as shown below. Iron the fold, taking care not to melt the fur with an overheated iron.

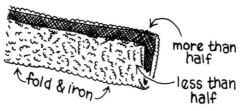

Starting at any point around the edge, pin one strip of shearling to the felt circle, slipping the felt all the way into the folded strip. The narrower "half" of the strip *must* be on top. When you have pinned all the way to the end of one strip simply butt another shearling strip next to the first strip and keep on pinning. Do not overlap the

MATERIALS

Circle of felt, 48″ in diameter, for the skirt (Be sure to buy high quality, color-fast felt)

Fake shearling fur ($\frac{1}{2}$ yd. if the fabric is 45″–60″ wide, $\frac{2}{3}$ yd. if the fabric is 36″ wide) **for the border**

1 piece of felt, $\frac{1}{2}$ yd. long and at least 42″ wide, for the bears (I used light brown for the bears but you may prefer another color. Choose one that contrasts with the skirt color)

Fusible web (like Stitch Witchery®), 18″ wide, one piece $1\frac{1}{4}$ yds. long

Plaid taffeta or other ribbon, $\frac{3}{8}$″ wide: 12 pieces, each 10″ long

Sequins: 12 medium (8 mm) **for the noses; 36 large** (10 mm) **for the eyes and mouths; 96 extra-large** (12 mm) **for the paws**

White glue

ends of the strips—overlapping would make the layers too thick to sew through.

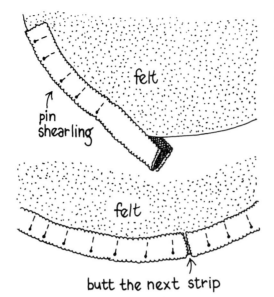

butt the next strip

Continue pinning the strips to the felt until you have worked all the way around the circle. Cut off the excess from the last strip, leaving a gap of $\frac{1}{2}''$ between the end of the last strip and the beginning of the first strip.

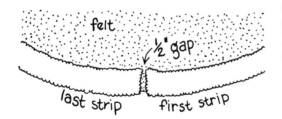

last strip   first strip

5 Topstitch the shearling strips to the felt circle, using a wide zigzag stitch right at the edge of the shearling. Because the narrower "half" is on top, the wider "half" underneath will also be securely sewed to the felt.

NOTE: When you are stitching, the fur may get caught in the presser foot. If this happens, carefully snip through the shearling or poke it out of the way and continue sewing.

6 Cut the brown felt into 12 rectangles, each 7″ × 9″, as shown below, saving the excess felt for another project. Do the same with the fusible web.

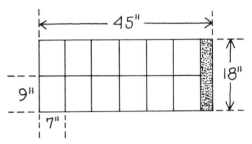

Outline the bear template on each rectangle of brown felt. Pin each piece of felt to a piece of fusible web, keeping the pins within the bear. Cut out each bear through both layers.

Now spread out the circle of felt flat on the floor. Space the 12 bears evenly around the circle, about 1″ from the shearling border, beginning to the left of the $\frac{1}{2}''$ gap in the fur and ending to the right of the gap. Pin each bear in position (two pins are enough) and heat-baste the bears to the tree

skirt. Remove all pins and fuse the bears securely to the skirt following the manufacturer's instructions.

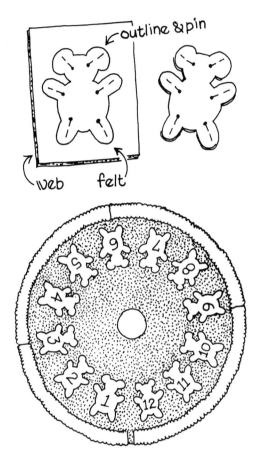

7 Put the finishing touches on the bears, using the photograph for guidance. Tie each piece of taffeta ribbon into a bow (see How to Tie a Bow, page 17), clip the ends on the diagonal and steam iron lightly to set. Glue each bow to the neck of a bear to make a bow tie.

Arrange sequins on one bear as shown in the drawing below, clipping off the top of a large sequin for the mouth. Pick up each sequin, apply a little white glue to the outer edge and replace on the bear. Let the glue dry. Repeat this procedure for all bears.

The glue holds the sequins in place temporarily. Now you must go back and *sew* the sequins to the felt, using a doubled piece of matching thread. To stitch each sequin, first knot the ends of thread together. Bring the needle up at the outer edge of a sequin and down into the center hole. Repeat two more times around the sequin to hold it securely.

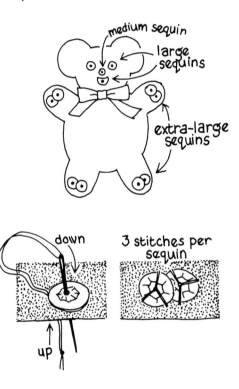

Finally, cut all the way across the felt at the $\frac{1}{2}''$ gap in the fur border. Wrap the skirt around the base of your tree.

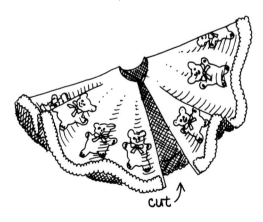

Paper Chains

This project makes use of all those leftover pieces of gift wrap you've been squirreling away—perhaps a combination of prints, solids and geometric patterns as well as birthday, baby shower and Father's Day papers. And don't forget Christmas gift wraps!

1 Cut the heavy paper or thin board into strips 6″ wide.

2 Lay several sheets of newspaper on the floor, place a strip in the center and spray with adhesive, following the manufacturer's instructions. Immediately, while the glue is still tacky, place the strip glue side down on the wrong side of a piece of gift wrap paper. Turn the two papers over and smooth the gift wrap firmly over the strip. Cut away the excess gift wrap.

4 The rest is child's play—and children love to do it, so let them help. Form one narrow strip into a ring and staple the overlap. Slip another strip in the ring and staple it closed. Continue in this manner until your chain is about 6-8 feet long. *Tip:* Don't try to make a chain long enough to go around the whole tree from top to bottom. Three or four shorter chains are much easier to handle. Do make a long chain to drape around a banister or doorway.

MATERIALS

Assorted gift wraps (If the papers are wrinkled, iron them flat with a dry iron set at low heat)

Heavy paper or thin board (Art Board, card stock, file folders, 2-ply Bristol board)

Spray adhesive

Small stapler

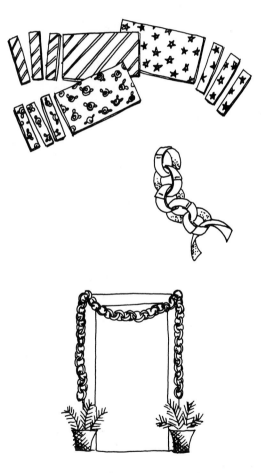

3 Cut the laminated papers into narrow strips, about $\frac{3}{4}$″ wide. Don't bother to measure the strips—just estimate by eye.

Teddy Bear Stockings (page 115)

Teddy Bear Stocking

1 Enlarge the stocking pattern on page 116 to make a template: Cut a piece of heavy paper 10″ × 16″ and mark it off in 1″ squares. Working square by square, copy the pattern above onto the corresponding squares on your grid. Cut out the enlarged stocking on the outline. Use this full-size heavy paper stocking as a template or, if you are making more than one or two stockings, outline the full-size paper stocking on thin cardboard to make a sturdier template.

2 Transfer and make a template from the small bear pattern shown on page 94, following the instructions on page 15.

3 Outline the bear template on the 5″ × 7″ piece of felt. Pin the felt to the piece of fusible web, keeping the pins within the bear. Cut out the bear on the outline, through both layers.

  Outline the stocking template on one 10″ × 17″ piece of felt. Position the bear within the stocking outline, centered 5½″ from the top of the stocking, and pin the bear to the stocking.

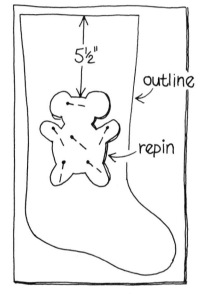

Heat-baste the bear to the stocking, remove all the pins and then fuse securely, following the manufacturer's instructions. *Tip:* Use a press-cloth in case your felt is not perfectly color-fast.

MATERIALS

2 pieces of felt, each 10″ × 17″, for the stocking

One piece of felt, 5″ × 7″ for the bear (I like light brown felt for the bear; if you prefer another color, choose one that contrasts with the stocking color)

Fusible web, one piece 5″ × 7″

Ribbon, $\frac{1}{4}$″ wide, one piece 8″ long for the bow tie

Sequins: 4 extra-large (12 mm) for the paws; one large (10 mm) for the mouth; 2 medium (8 mm) for the eyes; one small (6 mm) for the nose

Fake shearling fur, one piece 15″ × 4½″ for the cuff

Ribbon, $\frac{5}{8}$″ wide, one piece 5″ long for the loop

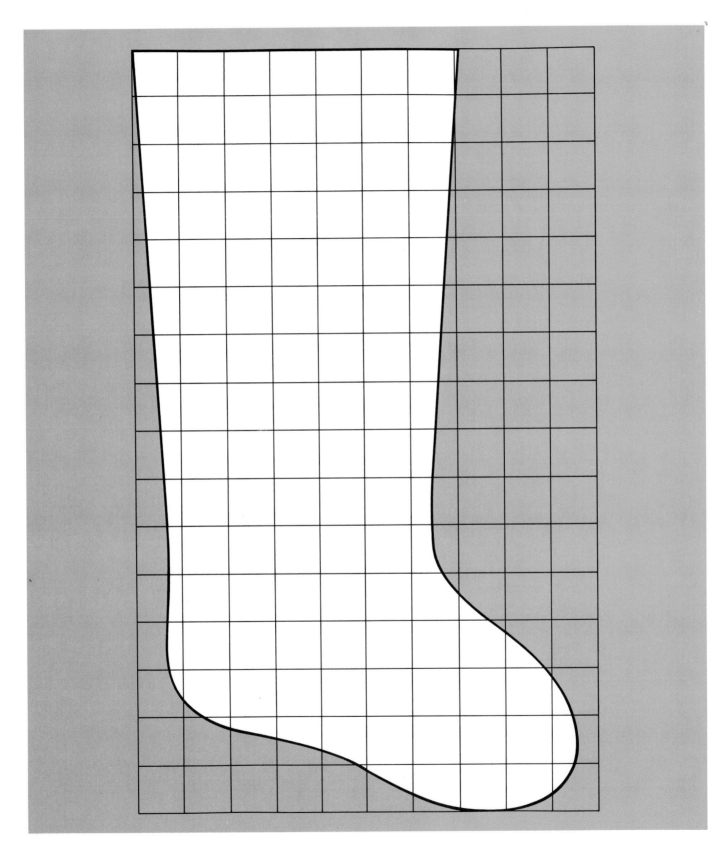

116

4 Decorate the bear, using the photograph on page 114 for guidance. Tie the $\frac{1}{4}$″-wide ribbon in a bow (see How to Tie a Bow, page 17) and tack it firmly to the bear's neck to make a bow tie. Clip the ends of the ribbon neatly on the diagonal.

Sew extra-large sequins to the bear for paws, a clipped large sequin for the mouth, two medium sequins for the eyes and one small sequin for the nose.

5 Pin the two pieces of felt together, with the outlined stocking on top. Using a tight zigzag, stitch the pieces together on the outline *except* on the straight line across the top. Carefully cut off the excess felt just outside the zigzag stitching and straight across the top on the outline.

6 Fold the piece of shearling fur in half with right sides together and straight-stitch the ends on a diagonal as shown. Steam iron the seam allowance open with iron set at low heat. Turn the cuff right side out. Turn under the lower edge (the wider edge) about $\frac{1}{2}$″ and topstitch.

NOTE: The fur tends to catch in the presser foot. When this happens, carefully clip the fur or poke it out of the way of the foot.

7 Slip the shearling cuff into the stocking, right side of cuff to wrong side of stocking. Match the seam of the cuff to the heel-side seam of the stocking and line up the narrower edge of the cuff with the top edge of the stocking. Stitch around the top of the stocking $\frac{1}{2}$″ from the edge.

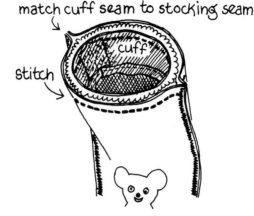

Turn the cuff up and out, folding it over at the new seam. Steam iron lightly around the top edge.

8 To make the loop, fold the $\frac{5}{8}$″-wide ribbon in half and tack the ends inside the stocking at the heel-side seam.

117

Painted Cookies (page 119)

Painted Cookies

These painted cookies are a craft project, not a cooking project. Decorator's Icing, which is used for decorating the cookies, is not very delicious to eat. It is important, therefore, to bake extra cookies to eat unpainted or frosted with a tasty buttercream.

1 Mix your cookie recipe, chill the dough and roll it out. Cut several of each cookie shape. Using a plastic straw, make a hole at the top of each cookie.

Bake the cookies until they are just golden. Don't let them get too brown; brightly colored icing shows up much better on light cookies than on dark ones. Let the cookies cool and then brush off any crumbs.

2 Make a batch of Decorator's Icing according to the recipe above, keeping it covered with plastic wrap as described.

To make each color, first put about two tablespoons of white icing in a small bowl or in one cup of a small muffin tin. Start adding drops of water and mixing until the icing is a little thicker than heavy cream. It should flow smoothly from a paint brush onto a cookie. Test the consistency as you dilute the icing.

Now dip a toothpick into one of the paste colors, scoop up a bit of paste and mix the color into the diluted white icing. Stir it vigorously and thoroughly. Paste color is very concentrated so only a bit is needed to get a rich tone. You'll see what I mean when you have mixed one or two colors.

Make all the colors you anticipate needing, keeping each one covered with a small piece of plastic wrap. With all the colors prepared you'll enjoy the painting much more, switching easily from one color to another, only stopping to rinse the brush in clean water between colors.

The colored icings will last several days, in or out of the refrigerator. Be sure to mix each color briskly before using it, adding a bit of undiluted white icing if the colored icing has become slightly watery overnight.

3 Paint the cookies, using the photograph as a guide or inventing your own designs. Here are some tips and pointers:

- Let the icing flow from the brush, but don't load the brush so much that it drips.

- Remember to rinse the brush in a jar of clean water when you change colors. Dry the brush on paper towels.

- Let each color dry on the cookie before applying another color either on top of it or adjacent to it.

- Work a bit like an assembly line: paint all the red hats on the Santas and set them aside to dry; paint the red stripes on several candy canes and set them aside; paint some little houses red and set them aside, too. By now the red hats should be dry. Go back and paint the white edgings on the hats and white beards and moustaches on the Santas' faces. Then paint the white stripes on the candy canes and the white roofs on the little houses.

MATERIALS

One or 2 recipes of your favorite rolled sugar cookies (The number of cookies you make depends on the size of your tree and how many cookies you want for munching)

Cookie cutters: traditional shapes like a candy cane, Santa's head, stocking, Christmas tree, bell; other shapes like a teddy bear, cow, duck, little house

Plastic drinking straws

Decorator's Icing (recipe follows)

Paste food coloring: red, royal blue, bright yellow, bright green (optional: orange and purple)

Small paint brushes

Crochet cord or string for the loops

DECORATOR'S ICING

$2\frac{1}{2}$-3 cups of confectioners' sugar

2 egg whites

$\frac{1}{4}$ teaspoon cream of tartar

In a large bowl stir the ingredients until blended. With an electric mixer, beat the mixture until it is stiff. This should take up to five minutes. Remember to scrape down the sides of the bowl. Cover with plastic wrap, pressing the wrap directly onto the surface of the icing. This prevents a crust from forming.

4 Attach a 16″ piece of cord or string to each cookie, as shown below. Tie the cookie to the tree with a bow.

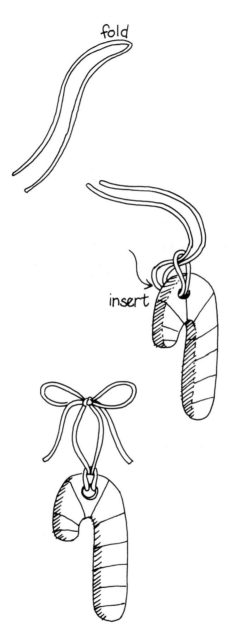

fold

insert

VARIATIONS

If you enjoy painting cookies, you might like to try some other ideas:

1. Bake and paint some giant cookies. A big Christmas tree would be fun.

2. Trim a small, live tree with hearts tied on with satin ribbon.

3. Make a cookie tree with an animal theme: Cut out horses, cows, chicks, bears and other creatures; paint them in crazy colors with dots and stripes for decoration.

4. Make a batch of large star-shaped cookies. Paint each one white, let it dry and add the name of a family member or friend.

6

Folk Art Ornaments

There are two tree-trimming schemes here—one with a natural, Scandinavian look (see the tree on page 122) and a second, on page 130, with a colorful Mexican style.

The Scandinavian ornaments look most pleasing when they are placed in an open but orderly arrangement, with gold garlands and white lights to set them off—you can see, for instance, that the Wheat and Wildflower Bouquet is a large ornament—each one needs some space around it to be most effective.

The Mexican-style tree is just the opposite. Hang these ornaments in a random and riotous profusion, mixing the colors, shapes and sizes. Notice that the green tree is a particularly good background for gold, pink and bright red.

Swedish Star

MATERIALS

One piece of #14 mono needlepoint canvas, 5″ × 5″

3-strand crewel yarn

2 blunt needles with large eyes

Don't be afraid to make this ornament even if you have never done needlepoint. There are no fancy techniques involved—just simple straight stitches made with yarn on needlepoint canvas.

Cut two pieces of yarn, each 34″ long. Divide them into six strands. Thread each needle with two strands of yarn, saving the remaining two strands for another star or another project.

Stitch the star following the diagram. The yarn in one needle will be enough to complete two sections of the star. End off and conceal the yarn ends on the back of the star.

Cut out the star with a sharp-pointed scissors, following the line indicated on the diagram. Be sure to count the canvas threads and holes carefully.

To make the loop, thread a needle with one short strand of yarn. Make a large knot near one end of the yarn. Bring the needle up through one point of the star and down through another point as shown below. The loop should be about 5″ long. Make another large knot at the back of the star and clip off the excess yarn.

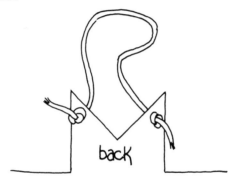

back

start

start

cut

125

Rope Heart

MATERIALS

Sisal rope, ⅜″ in diameter: made up of 3 strands, 2 pieces, each 9″ long

Thin wire or string

Grosgrain ribbon, ⅜″ wide: one small piece for tying the lower end of the heart; one piece 18″ long for the bow

1 Unwind the pieces of rope into six separate strands. Fasten the six strands together securely with thin wire or string, about 1½″ from the ends. Carefully braid three strands, keeping the braid as flat as you can. Braid the remaining three strands in the same way. The flat sides should be back to back. NOTE: The ends of the rope will probably unravel somewhat; this is perfectly fine.

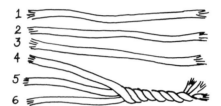

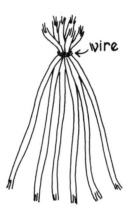

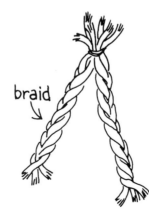

2 Hold the tied end of the braids pointing down and bend the braids around to form a heart. Pinch the ends together and secure them by wrapping with wire or tying with string.

3 Tie a small piece of grosgrain ribbon over the string or wire at the lower end of the heart, knotting it firmly in back. Clip the ends of ribbon on the diagonal. Tie the 18″ piece of ribbon over the wire or string at the upper end of the heart to make a pretty bow on the front. Clip the ends of ribbon on the diagonal.

The heart needs no special loop. Hang it on the tree by slipping a branch through the heart as shown in the photograph on page 122.

Wheat and Wildflower Bouquet

1 Group four or five different stems of flowers in a pretty bunch and wrap the piece of wire around them tightly two or three times. Twist the wire at the back to secure.

Gather the wheat stalks together behind the flowers. Wrap the wire once around the wheat stalks and then several times around the entire bouquet. Twist the wire ends together tightly in back of the bouquet. Clip off any excess wire.

2 Prepare the four pieces of 14″-long ribbon: Fold each piece in half and stack the pieces neatly with all the folds at the top. Hold the pieces at a point $2\frac{3}{4}$″ from the folds and fan them out as shown. Tack the pieces together with needle and thread.

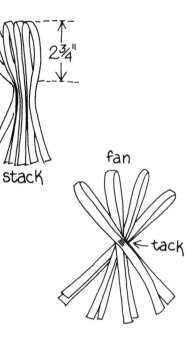

3 Place the ribbon fan on top of the flower/wheat bouquet, matching the tacking stitches and the wire. Tie them together with the 10″ piece of ribbon, covering the

MATERIALS

4 or 5 stems of fabric flowers (Choose four or five different kinds of small wildflowers like daisies, cornflowers and buttercups. Each stem should have several flowers and leaves on it; cut the stem into 4″ sections as shown below. This will give you enough flowers to make four or five ornaments)

10″ piece of florist's wire (This is a thin, very flexible green wire packed on a spool)

5 stalks of wheat with stems cut to 6″ long

Scraps of grosgrain and satin ribbon in bright colors: 4 pieces, each 14″ long, in widths of $\frac{1}{8}$″, $\frac{1}{4}$″ and/or $\frac{3}{8}$″; one piece 10″ long, $\frac{1}{8}$″ wide

Grosgrain ribbon, $\frac{1}{8}$″ wide, one piece 14″ long for the loop

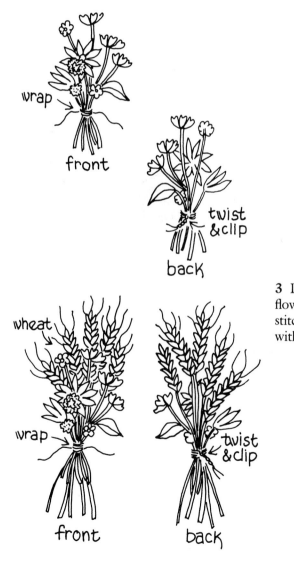

green wire, knotting the ribbon tightly on the front of the bouquet. Clip the ends of all the ribbons on the diagonal, varying the lengths slightly.

4 Turn the bundle over to the back. Tie the 14″ piece of $\frac{1}{8}$″ wide grosgrain just under one of the heads of wheat. When you hang the ornament on the tree, rest the wheat stalks across a branch or two and tie the ribbon ends to another branch to help anchor and balance the ornament.

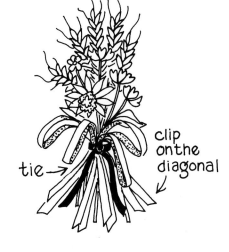

tie →

clip on the diagonal ↓

tie →

back

Mexican Lantern

1 Carefully cut the rim away from the cookie sheet, leaving a flat piece 14″ × 9″. Cut the flat piece into four quarters, each 4½″ × 7″.

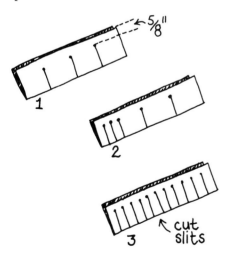

2 Work with one quarter to make one lantern. Fold the piece of aluminum in half lengthwise and cut 11 slits as shown in the drawing. Leave an uncut edge about ⅝″ wide.

NOTE: There is no need to measure before cutting the slits. This ornament should look somewhat imperfect, in the folk art spirit.

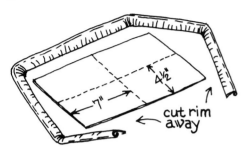

3 Carefully unfold the aluminum and press it over the edge of a table to set the shape correctly. Fold each edge over the table as well, making creases just at the end of the slits.

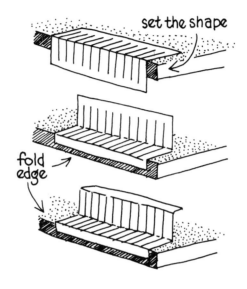

4 Place the lantern flat on the table as shown. Paint squares of color along both edges, alternating red and blue: paint all the red squares first, allow them to dry and then paint the blue squares. Let the blue dry.

Now rest the lantern on a box or a block of wood and paint the uppermost half of each narrow strip yellow. Let the paint dry. Turn the lantern around, paint the other

MATERIALS

Disposable aluminum cookie sheet, 15″ × 10⅜″ (You can make four lanterns from one cookie sheet)

Acrylic glass stain paints: red, blue and yellow (These are translucent, water-soluble paints which simulate the look of stained glass. They are available at hobby or craft supply stores and many art supply stores)

Paint brush

Stapler, hole puncher

Gold cord, one piece 7″ long for the loop of each lantern

halves yellow and let the paint dry. Repeat once more for a richer color.

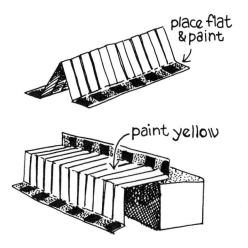

place flat & paint

paint yellow

5 When the paint is completely dry, bend the top and bottom edges into circles, overlapping one square. Staple the overlaps. The narrow strips will automatically fan out into the correct lantern shape. Make the lantern wider or narrower by pressing the top edge down or pulling it up.

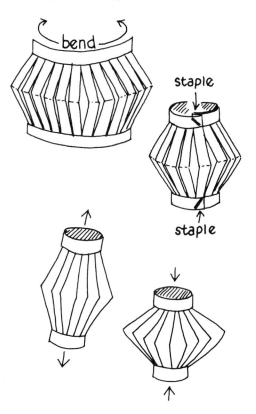

bend

staple

staple

6 Punch holes opposite each other in the top edge. To make the loop, first tie a big knot near the end of a 7″ piece of gold cord. Thread the unknotted end through both holes and tie another knot as shown below.

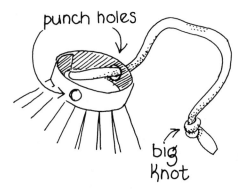

punch holes

big knot

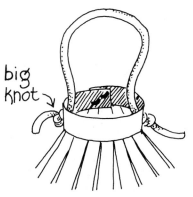

big knot

Silver Bell

MATERIALS

Disposable aluminum cookie sheet, 15″ × 10⅜″ (You can make several bells from one cookie sheet)

Thin-pointed felt tip marker

Acrylic glass stain paints: blue and either magenta or red (These are translucent, water-soluble paints which simulate the look of stained glass. They are available at hobby or craft supply stores and many art supply stores)

Paint brush

Stapler, hole puncher

Silver cord or soutache, one piece 12″ long for the loop

1 Transfer the bell pattern to heavy paper or thin cardboard to make a template according to the instructions on page 15.

Carefully cut the rim away from the bottom of the cookie sheet, leaving a flat piece about 14″ × 9″. With the felt tip marker, outline the template twice on the aluminum. (Outline the template twice more for each additional bell you want to make.) Cut out both bells with an ordinary scissors.

2 Use red or magenta to paint one side of each bell as shown in the drawing, leaving a silver rim. Let the paint dry, then paint blue dots on the silver rim. When the blue paint is completely dry, turn the bells over and repeat. Allow the paint to dry.

3 Place one bell on top of the other and staple them together in three places with the staples running vertically. Punch a hole in the top, through both bells. Bend the bells apart so the four sections are at right angles to each other.

4 To make the loop, slip the cord or soutache through the punched hole and tie the bell to the tree with a bow.

132

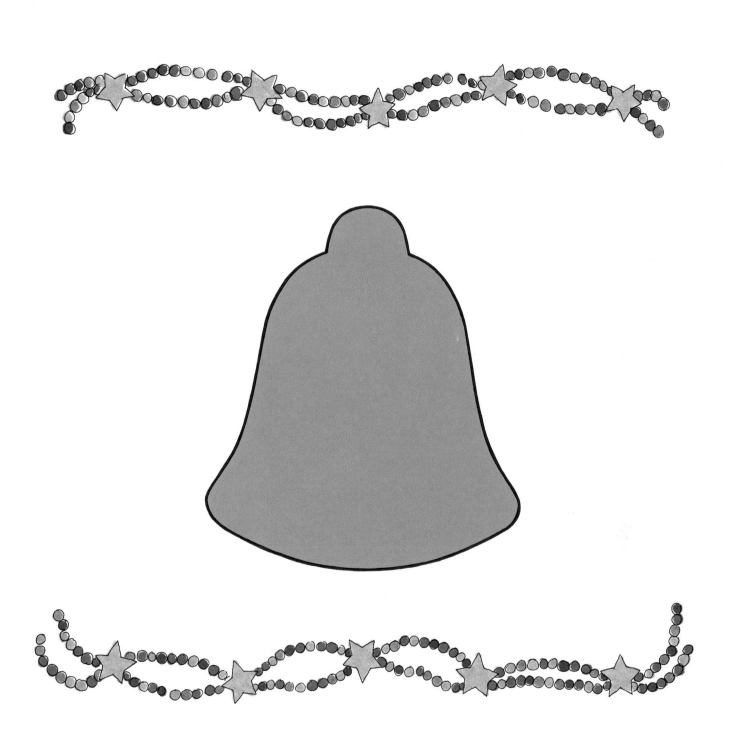

Mexican Garlands

MATERIALS

Brightly colored tissue paper (Buy a package of assorted colors or several sheets each of six or eight colors)

One package of plastic drinking straws (*not* the flexible kind); one package of 48 straws will make 3 garlands, each 10 ft. long

Thin string or crochet thread, 3 pieces each 12 ft. long

6 medium or large buttons

Large needle

Sharp-pointed scissors

These garlands are beautiful on the Christmas tree (see the photograph on page 130), but you might also drape several of them around a doorway or bay window or even across the room to make festive party decorations.

1 Cut each straw into three approximately equal pieces.

2 Fold six sheets of the same color tissue paper in quarters to make a stack 24 sheets thick. You will be cutting through all 24 sheets at the same time.

Cut the sheets into 2″ squares. Cut the corners off each little stack of squares. At each point cut out a wedge. You now have a stack of 24 flowers.

Divide the stack of 24 flowers into three piles of eight.

Repeat this process with all the colors you have chosen. You will need 50-55 piles of eight flowers for each 10-foot garland, so make about 160 piles for the whole project. This sounds like a formidable number, but remember that you are making not one but three piles at a time.

3 Tie a button to one end of one piece of string and put the other end through the eye of the needle. Thread a piece of plastic straw on the needle, then a pile of eight tissue paper flowers. Continue threading straws and flowers, alternating the colors, until you have only 1½ feet of string left. Be sure to end with a straw. Tie a button to this end and clip off the excess string.

Repeat step 3 to make two more garlands.

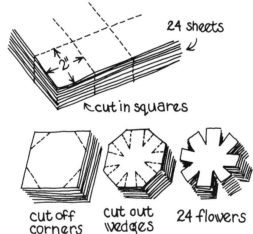

24 sheets

2″

cut in squares

cut off corners

cut out wedges

24 flowers

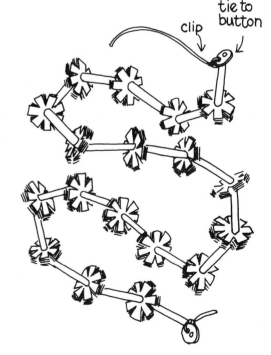

tie to button

clip

Dragonfly

1 Transfer the wing pattern to heavy paper or thin cardboard to make a template according to the instructions on page 15.

2 Cut a 3″ piece of Color A. Roll it up lengthwise, moisten the edge and press it down to make a flattened tube. Snip the ends to points to make the body.

Cut a ¾″ piece of Color B and snip off four narrow strips. Moisten the end of each strip and slip each one into the tube as shown below to make the antennae and tail.

3 Cut a 10″ piece of Color B and fold it into quarters. Outline the wing template on the top quarter and cut on the outline through all four layers to make four wings.

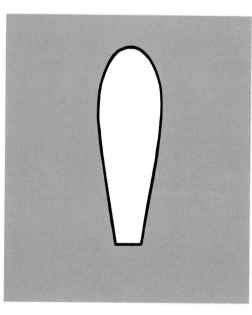

MATERIALS

2 contrasting colors of gift wrap ribbon (Color A and Color B), ¾″ wide, labeled "sticks to itself when lightly moistened" (You can use any gift wrap ribbon plus glue to make this ornament, but part of the fun of making it is in taking advantage of the self-sticking ribbon)

Gold thread

Transparent tape

4 Cut an 8″ piece of Color A and fold it in quarters. Without bothering to cut a pattern or template, draw the wing trim on the top quarter and cut on the outline through all four layers.

Moisten the back of each wing trim and place it on the *wrong* side (the glue-coated side) of one wing.

5 Put the wing sections together as shown below to make the whole wing unit. Moist-en the center of the wing unit and press the dragonfly body in position on it.

6 Cut an 8″ piece of gold thread, fold it in half and tape the ends to the back of the dragonfly. Position the ends as shown so the dragonfly will hang on an angle.

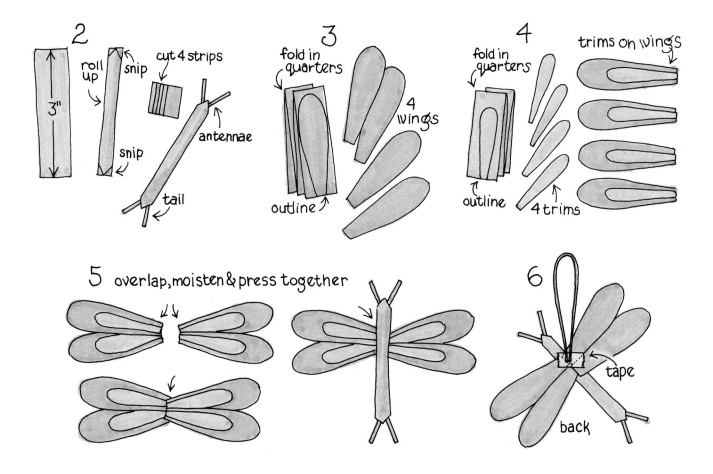

Paper Snowflake

1 Pick a bright color of origami paper and fold it in half so only the white side shows. Find the midpoint of the folded edge, fold the paper in thirds and cut off the excess as shown in the drawing below.

Now you have a folded stack of six wedges.

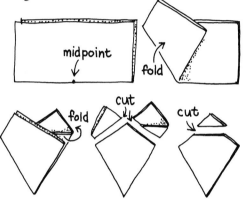

2 Draw a design on the top of the stack, using one of the patterns above or inventing your own. *Tip:* To transfer one of the patterns to the origami paper, first place a piece of tracing paper over the pattern.

Then trace all the lines (including the outline) with a very soft pencil. Turn the tracing paper *over* and place it on the folded origami paper, matching the outline to the edges of the origami paper. Draw over the pencil lines with a ball point pen or a hard pencil. Lift the tracing paper and you will see that the design has been transferred.

With a soft pencil, darken the areas to be cut out so you don't get confused. Cut them out with a sharp-pointed scissors, through all layers of paper.

3 Unfold the snowflake very carefully. Press out the creases by ironing it with a dry iron set at low heat, with a piece of smooth paper between the iron and the snowflake.

4 Spread a few sheets of newspaper on the floor and place the snowflake wrong side up on them. Spray the snowflake with the

MATERIALS

Origami paper, one piece 4½″ square

Heavy weight colored paper or thin board (Art Board, oaktag, poster board, etc.), one piece 6″ square

Sharp-pointed scissors

Spray adhesive

Hole puncher

Cord, one piece 12″ long for the loop

spray adhesive, following the manufacturer's instructions. While the glue is still tacky, put the snowflake (adhesive side down) on the heavy weight colored paper, cover it with a piece of scrap paper and rub firmly with the palm of your hand to encourage its smooth, even adherence.

5 Cut away the excess heavy weight paper just outside the snowflake, leaving a thin rim of the contrasting color all the way around the origami paper.

To make the loop, punch a hole in the snowflake near the edge and attach the cord as shown. Tie the ends of the cord to the tree, making a small bow.

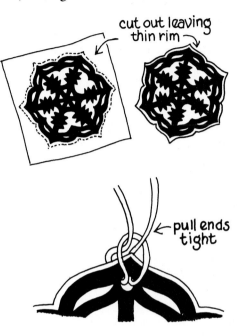

cut out leaving thin rim

pull ends tight

Golden Angel

When you look at the close-up photograph above or the tree on page 140, you may not realize that the Golden Angels are made of paper. In fact, each angel starts out as two flat pieces—the body and the wings—which only take shape when you bend, score, fold and glue them.

1 Transfer the body pattern (page 142) and the wings pattern to heavy paper or thin board to make templates, as explained on page 15. Be sure to transfer the cutting lines and the scoring lines as well as the outlines.

2 Outline the templates on the white side of the gold paper. For each angel you must outline the body template once and the wings template once.

If you are making several angels, map out a paper-saving arrangement first by moving the templates around on the paper until you arrive at the most economical plan. Cut out the pieces on the outlines and along the cutting lines.

3 Make the angel's body.

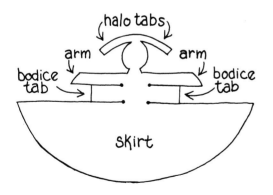

Skirt: Gently bend the skirt into a cone shape, gold side out, overlapping the ends 3″ in back as shown. The bottom edges should be even. Glue the overlap in this position, using clips or clothespins to hold it while the glue dries.

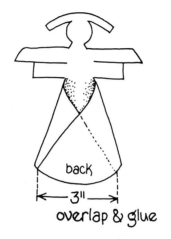

Use glue sparingly. It should be tacky and not runny when you press two parts together. Glue that oozes onto the gold paper will dry with a matte finish and ruin the gleaming look of your angel, so wipe away excess glue with a slightly dampened soft cloth.

Bodice: Bend the bodice tabs around to the back of the angel. Overlap them about $\frac{1}{2}$″ at a slight angle and glue them in position. Clip while the glue dries if necessary.

MATERIALS

Heavy weight gold paper (This paper is usually gold on one side and white on the other. It is sold in standard-size sheets, each of which will yield several angels if you place your templates efficiently)

Mat knife or X-acto® knife

Metal ruler

One package of self-adhesive gold craft trim or one piece of narrow gold trim, 26″ long

White glue

Golden Angel (page 139)

Arms: Curve the arms forward and down. Overlap at the wrists and glue in position.

Halo: Bend the halo tabs forward, rounding them. Overlap about $\frac{1}{4}$"-$\frac{3}{8}$" and glue in position. Hold for a few seconds while the glue dries.

back   front

4 Glue (or press into position, if you are using self-adhesive trim) a small piece of gold trim around the halo, clipping off any excess to make the ends butt perfectly at the back of the halo. Glue another small piece of gold trim at the wrist overlap. Using the close-up photograph for guidance, glue gold trim around the lower edge of the skirt, one piece about $\frac{1}{2}$" above the other. Make the ends of each piece of trim meet perfectly in the back.

5 Score the wings and attach them to the angel: Use the X-acto® knife or mat knife and metal ruler to score the wings lightly on the white side of the paper on the indicated scoring lines. Fold the wings gently on the scored lines. Turn the wings over to

the gold side and score again between the folds, two new scores per wing. There is no need to measure or draw lines for this.

Fold on the new scored lines.

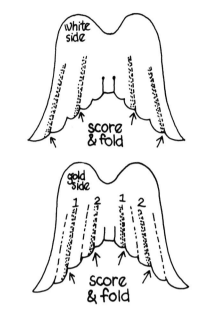

Put glue sparingly on the overlapped bodice tabs and center the wings on the glue with the gold side touching the bodice tabs. Clip in position with a clothespin by coming up from the bottom inside the skirt. Secure the wings at the top with a hair clip if necessary, while the glue dries.

Balance each angel among the branches of your tree or, if the tree is artificial, bend the tip of a branch up into the skirt to hold the angel more securely.

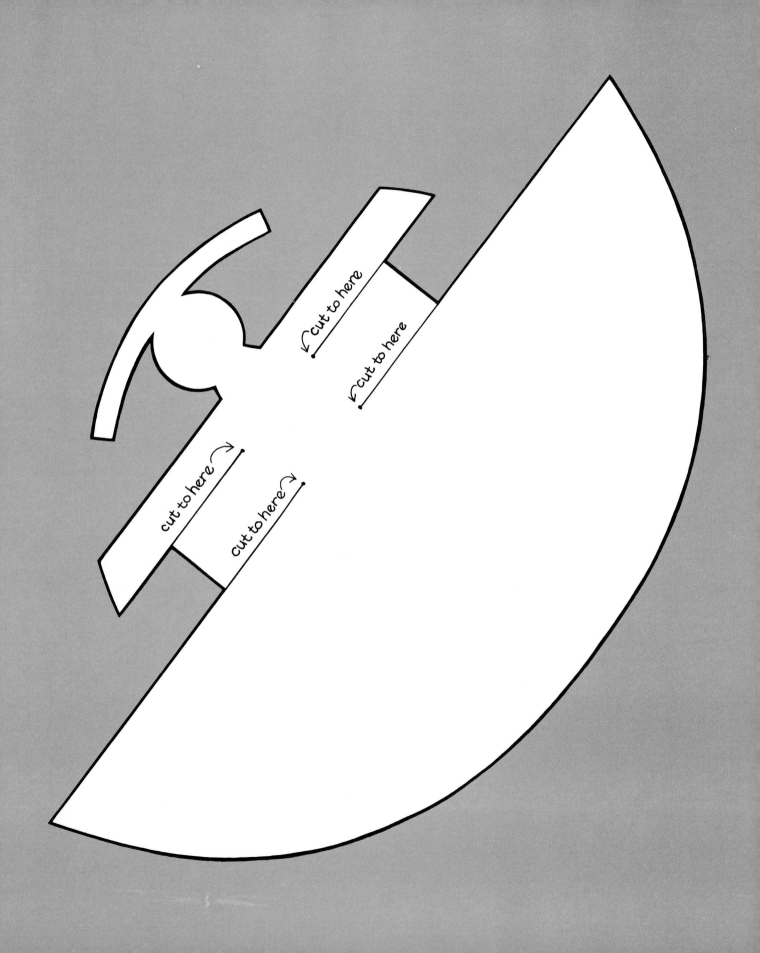

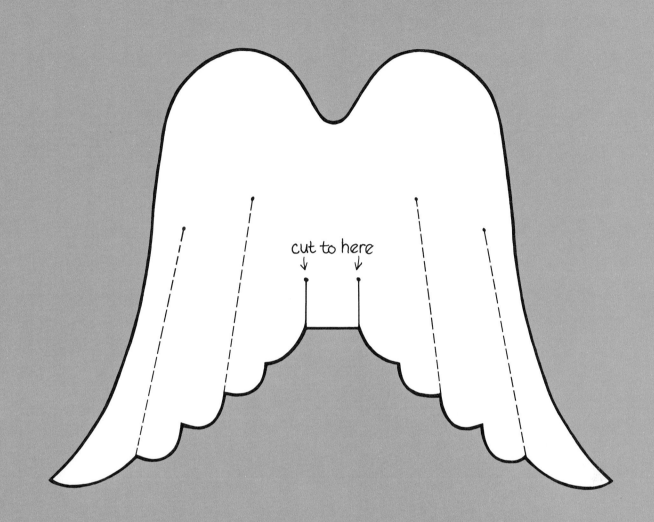

Mexican Lanterns (page 129), Tyrolean
Angels (page 145)

Tyrolean Angel

A trio of angels looks lovely on a mantel or sideboard, as shown in the photograph on page 144, and one angel is perfect for the top of your tree.

1 Transfer the body pattern and the wings pattern of the Golden Angel, pages 142 and 143, to heavy paper or thin cardboard to make templates as explained on page 15. Transfer the underskirt pattern and the apron pattern (page 147), using the same method. Be sure to transfer all the cutting lines and scoring lines.

Outline the body template on the wrong side of one color of paper. Outline the apron and underskirt templates on the wrong side of the second color of paper. Outline the wings template on the wrong side of the white paper.

Cut out all the pieces on the outlines and on the cutting lines.

2 Glue the apron to the right side of the angel's skirt, centering it as shown. Trim the apron and skirt with Color A of baby rickrack, cutting the pieces to fit and attaching them with white glue. Use a toothpick to apply glue to the back of each piece of rickrack.

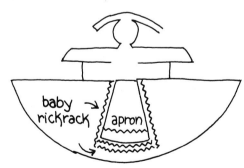

Shape the underskirt into a partial cone as shown, right side out, overlapping the ends 1¼″ in back. Glue the overlap in position, clip with a clothespin and let dry.

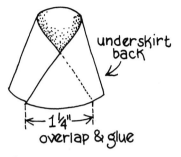

3 Make the angel's body:

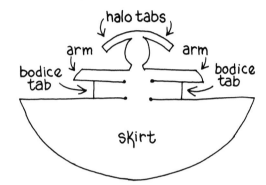

Skirt: Gently bend the skirt into a cone shape, right side out, overlapping the ends 3″ in back as shown. Glue the overlap in position and clip it with a clothespin while the glue dries.

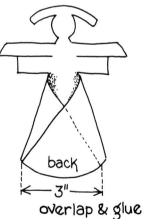

Bodice: Bend the bodice tabs around to the back of the angel. Overlap about ½″ at a slight angle and glue in position. Glue the

MATERIALS

Heavy paper or thin board in two contrasting colors (Use bright colors. Try the combinations in the photograph on page 144—blue and yellow, red and yellow, green and yellow—or perhaps you might like bright pink and light blue, orange and green or traditional red and green)

Heavy white paper or thin white board

Scraps of the following trims (use photograph for guidance):
Baby rickrack in two colors (Color A and Color B) to contrast with the colored paper
Loop braid, one piece 12″ long
Embroidered ribbon, ¾″ wide, one piece 4″ long
Ruffled eyelet, 1″ wide, one piece 12″ long

Dried flowers, a few sprigs for the bouquet

X-acto® knife or mat knife, metal ruler

White glue

piece of embroidered ribbon over the bodice, ending neatly in back.

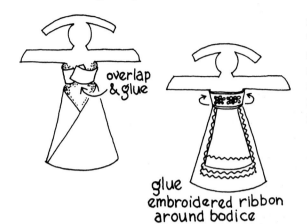

overlap & glue

glue embroidered ribbon around bodice

overlap & glue

Arms: Curve the arms forward and down. Overlap at the wrists and glue in position.

Halo: Bend the halo tabs forward, rounding them. Overlap about $\frac{1}{4}''$-$\frac{3}{8}''$ and glue in position.

4 Place the angel on the underskirt to see where the points of contact will be. Take the angel off, dab glue on the underskirt at those points and replace the angel. Clip with clothespins while the glue dries, if necessary.

5 Decorate the angel, following the photograph for guidance. Using Color B, glue baby rickrack around the lower edge of the underskirt and around the halo. NOTE: All trims begin and end at the back of the angel. Cut the ends of each piece of trim so they meet without overlapping.

Glue ruffled eyelet around the angel's skirt (not the underskirt). Glue the loop braid over the eyelet, with the heading of the loop braid on the heading of the eyelet.

Make a small bouquet of a few dried flowers, breaking off the stems to about $2\frac{1}{2}''$ long. Place the flowers in the arms of the angel and dab a bit of glue on the arms at the points of contact. This will hold the flowers in place.

6 Using Color A, glue rickrack to each wing as shown.

Use the X-acto® knife or mat knife and metal ruler to score the wings lightly on the wrong side of the paper, on the indicated scoring lines. Fold the wings gently on the scored lines. Turn the wings over to the right side and score again between the folds, two new scores per wing. There is no need to measure or draw lines for this.

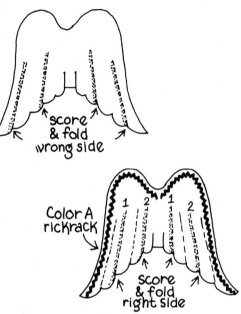

score & fold wrong side

Color A rickrack

score & fold right side

Fold on the new scored lines.

Put glue sparingly on the embroidered ribbon on the back of the angel and center the wings on the glue with the right side touching the ribbon. Clip in position with a clothespin coming up from the bottom, inside the skirt. Secure the wings at the top with a hair clip, if necessary, while the glue dries.

back

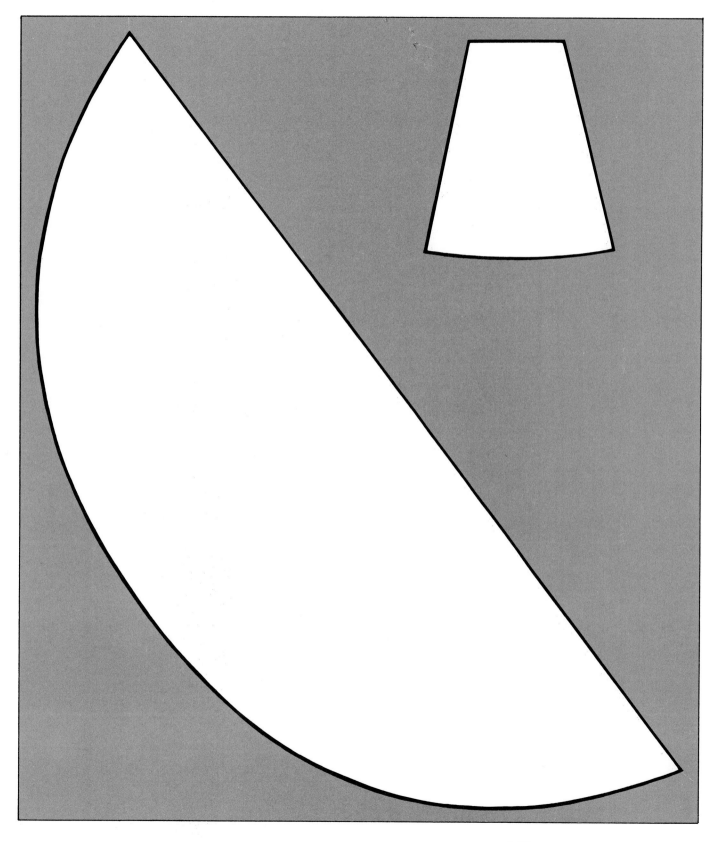

147

7
Natural Ornaments

The charm of these ornaments is in their warm, earthy colors and in the use of natural materials like moss, dried flowers, cornhusks, cinnamon sticks, basswood and pinecones. But you certainly don't have to live in a forest to get your hands on any of these materials; they are all available in local stores or even in your own home. The Bread Dough Birds (page 157) are made from flour, salt and water!

And for the busy, thrifty craftsperson there are three special projects in this chapter: Pinecone Candleholders and Apple Candleholders which combine to make a mantel decoration (page 160) and a group of designs which turn plain store-bought or homemade pine wreaths into festive holiday decorations.

Frosted Pinecone

MATERIALS

Small pinecone, 1½″-2″ long
Salt
Thin wire, packed on a spool
White glue

Pour a little glue onto a piece of waxed paper. Pour salt into a small bowl.

With your finger, dab glue on the tips of the "petals" of the pinecone. Roll the pinecone in the bowl of salt to coat the tips generously. Set the pinecone aside until the glue dries, then tap off the excess salt.

Cut a 12″ piece of wire. Insert the end of the wire under a "petal" at the stem end of the pinecone and then wind the wire around two or three times, catching it under several of the "petals" so it is firmly anchored to the pinecone.

Attach the pinecone to the tree by positioning it on a branch and then wrapping the wire around the branch to hold the pinecone in place. If they are small and narrow, you might like to attach two pinecones at a time by twisting their wires together and then wrapping the double wire around the branch.

Basswood Star

1 With a coping saw, cut the following pieces of $\frac{1}{16}''$ thick basswood: Piece A, $\frac{1}{2}'' \times 3\frac{1}{2}''$; Piece B, $\frac{1}{2}'' \times 2\frac{3}{4}''$; Piece C, $\frac{1}{2}'' \times \frac{1}{2}''$; Pieces D and E, each $\frac{3}{8}'' \times 2\frac{3}{4}''$.

Sand all the cut edges lightly with fine sandpaper.

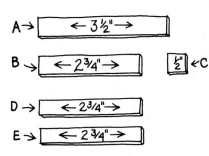

2 Drill a $\frac{3}{32}''$ hole near the top of Piece A. Sand, if necessary.

3 Mark the center $\frac{1}{2}''$ of Pieces A and B. Glue them together perpendicular to each other, matching up the marks, with A on top of B. Now mark the center $\frac{1}{2}''$ of Pieces D and E and glue them together in the same way, with D on top of E.

Glue the pairs together, matching up the centers, with A/B on top of D/E. Let the glue dry.

Glue Piece C (the little square) to the center of Piece A. This is the front. Let the glue dry thoroughly.

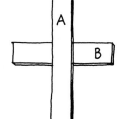

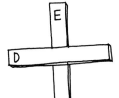

4 Brush polyurethane on the front of the star first and let it dry. Be careful not to clog the hole with polyurethane.

Turn the star over and brush polyurethane on the back. Let the polyurethane dry. Repeat the process for a second coat.

Clean the brush with turpentine and then with soap and water.

MATERIALS

Basswood strips: one strip $\frac{1}{16}''$ thick $\times$ $\frac{3}{8}''$ wide; one strip $\frac{1}{16}''$ thick $\times$ $\frac{1}{2}''$ wide (Buy basswood strips at any good art supply store or hobby and craft shop. The strips are generally 18″ long, which will provide you with enough to make two stars with some basswood left over)

Coping saw or any other thin-bladed saw

Fine sandpaper

Drill with a $\frac{3}{32}''$ bit

Satin-finish polyurethane

Brush, turpentine

Pearl cotton, one piece 14″ long for the loop

White glue

5 Thread the pearl cotton through the hole to make a loop as shown below. Tie the star to the tree, making a bow.

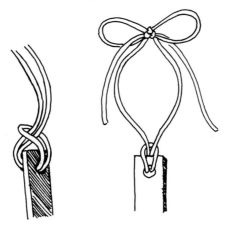

BASSWOOD STAR FOR THE TOP OF THE TREE

The treetop star is made exactly the same way as the ornament except that you do not drill a hole in Piece A. The lengths of the pieces are different, too: Piece A, $\frac{1}{2}'' \times 5''$; Piece B, $\frac{1}{2}'' \times 3\frac{3}{4}''$; Pieces D and E, each $\frac{3}{8}'' \times 3\frac{3}{4}''$. Piece C is the same, $\frac{1}{2}'' \times \frac{1}{2}''$.

Tuck the star in place at the top of the tree and fasten it with a piece of narrow tape across the back.

Cornhusk Wreath

1 Pick out six dried husks that have no tears or ragged edges. Soak the dried husks in the bowl of warm water for 15-30 minutes, until the husks are soft and pliable. Pat them with paper towels, blotting off the water but leaving the husks damp.

2 Place the wide (stem) ends of three husks together and wind thread around them tightly about 2″ from the ends, leaving long ends of thread.
  Braid the husks until there are about 2½″ left unbraided, curving the braid slightly as you work.

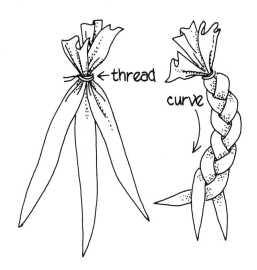

Add the remaining three husks, following the diagram carefully.

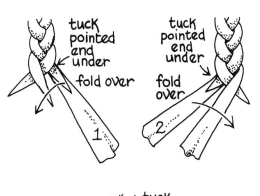

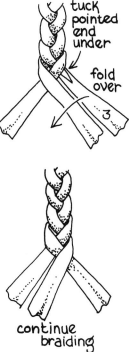

Continue braiding the added husks. Remember to curve the braid slightly as you work along. Stop when there are about 2½″ left unbraided.

MATERIALS

Dried cornhusks (Prepare dried cornhusks in the summer and fall. First strip the husks from several ears of corn, taking care not to split or break them. Then pick out only the inner husks—the outer ones are too stiff and thick—and spread them in a single layer on wire cookie or cake racks. They will dry in a day or two. Store them in a plastic bag until you are ready to use them. Be sure to prepare more than you will need so you'll have a choice of the best husks)

Bowl of warm water

White thread

Taffeta ribbon, ⅜″ wide, one piece 15″ long

9 dried flowers (Choose flowers with small, round heads; check the photograph on page 154 for guidance. Break off and discard the stems)

White glue

153

Cornhusk Wreath (page 153), Cinnamon
Bundle (page 156), Bread Dough Bird
(page 157)

3 Shape the braid into a ring with the un-braided ends overlapping as shown. Wind the long ends of thread tightly around the overlap and knot them on the back of the wreath. Clip off the excess thread.

Split the ends of the husks and then use a scissors to snip some of the ends on the diagonal, varying the lengths. Flatten the wreath by pressing it down firmly with the palm of your hand.

4 To make the loop, fold the taffeta ribbon in half and make a knot 3″ from the fold. Tie the ends of the ribbon around the wreath to cover the thread, knotting the ribbon in front. Snip the ends on the diagonal.

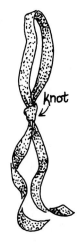

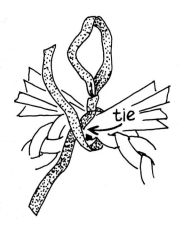

Let the wreath dry completely, either for a day or two on a cookie rack or for a few hours in a warm (but *turned off*) oven.

Glue the dried flowers to the front of the wreath as shown in the photograph. Use a tweezers to dip each flower in glue and place it on the wreath.

Cinnamon Bundle

4 cinnamon sticks, each 2½″ long (Buy cinnamon sticks at the supermarket or any fancy food store. They may come longer than 2½″ so cut them to size with a coping saw: score a shallow groove all around the stick at the correct length and break the stick on the scored line)

Thin wire, packed on a spool, one piece 12″ long

Taffeta ribbon, ⅝″ wide, one piece 14″ long for the bow

2 sprigs of dried flowers (Check the photograph on page 154 for guidance)

Grosgrain ribbon, ⅛″ wide, one piece 8″ long for the loop

White glue

1 Group the cinnamon sticks in a bundle with glue smeared between them. Grip the bundle firmly and wrap the thin wire twice around the center. Twist the wire ends together tightly to hold the bundle while the glue dries. When the glue is dry, snip through the wire and discard it. The bundle will hold together securely.

2 Tie the taffeta ribbon around the middle of the bundle and make a pretty bow, cutting the ends of the ribbon in points.

3 Dip the stem of one sprig of flowers in glue, position it to the left of the bow and insert the stem under the knot. Repeat with the second sprig, positioning it on the right side of the bow.

4 To make the loop, start by slipping the end of the grosgrain ribbon under the taffeta ribbon just above the bow. *Tip:* Poke it through with the point of a scissors. Tie the ends of the grosgrain ribbon in a tight knot. Pull the knot around until it is hidden under the taffeta ribbon.

pull knot around, under ribbon

Bread Dough Birds

FLOUR/SALT DOUGH
2 cups white flour
$\frac{1}{2}$ cup salt (iodized or plain)
$\frac{3}{4}$ cup water

In a bowl, mix the flour and salt until well blended. Add $\frac{1}{2}$ cup of water and continue mixing. Slowly add the remaining water while turning the dough to moisten it. Push the dough into a ball, working in any dry flour and salt left at the bottom of the bowl. Knead the dough on a floured surface for at least 10 minutes. *Tip:* Set your kitchen timer to remind you. Wrap the dough tightly in plastic.

Too-dry dough: If the dough cracks and splits at the edges when you are kneading it, it is too dry. To counteract the dryness, simply wet your hands and keep kneading, working the moisture into the dough. Repeat if necessary.

Too-moist dough: If the dough feels soft and weepy instead of firm and pliable, it is too moist. Mix a tablespoon of flour with a tablespoon of salt and dust your kneading surface with this mixture. As you knead, the flour and salt will be incorporated into the dough and they will absorb some of the moisture from the dough. Repeat if necessary.

Start this project by making three test birds to determine the placement of the loophole.

1 Break off a small piece of dough; rewrap the remaining dough tightly. Dust the table or countertop with flour and roll out the dough to a thickness of a little less than $\frac{1}{4}''$. Use the cookie cutter to cut out three birds. With the plastic straw, make one hole in each bird as shown—dead center, slightly left of center and slightly right of center.

center

left

right

Roll a bit of dough to a thickness of $\frac{1}{8}''$. Use the aspic cutter to cut out three wings. Dab a bit of water on the back of each wing to act as glue and position one wing

MATERIALS
One recipe of flour/salt dough (The recipe will yield about 12-15 birds, depending on the size of the bird)

Rolling pin

Cookie cutter in the shape of a small bird, about 3″ across

Aspic cutter in a diamond, tear or crescent shape for the wing

Plastic straw, toothpick

Spatula, cookie sheet

Stiff kitchen brush

Satin-finish polyurethane

Paint brush, turpentine

Pearl cotton, one piece 16″ long for each loop

on each bird as shown. Using the toothpick, make an eye in each bird.

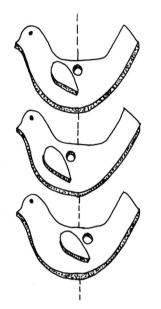

2 Lift each bird carefully with the spatula,
transfer it to a flour-dusted cookie sheet and
bake all three at 300° for 40 minutes. Turn
the birds over on the cookie sheet and bake
for 20 minutes more. At this point the
birds should be completely hard and lightly
browned. Remove them from the oven and
allow them to cool.

3 Make pearl cotton loops for all three
birds. Hold the ends of each loop and note
the bird that hangs straight.

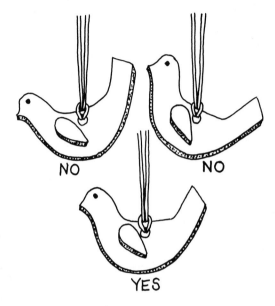

Use the remaining dough to make more
birds, repeating the basic process and making each hole in the correct position. When
the birds are baked and cooled, brush off
any excess flour with a stiff kitchen brush.

With the paint brush, apply a coat of polyurethane to the front and edges of each bird
and let dry on waxed paper. Turn the birds
over, apply a coat to the backs, and let dry.
Repeat the process a second time. Clean the
brush first with turpentine and then with
soap and water.

When all the birds are completely dry, add
the pearl cotton loops. Hang the birds on
the tree by tying the ends of the pearl cotton over the branches in bows.

Apple Candleholder

Polish the apple. Stand it up and insert the apple corer in the center, as perpendicular to the table as possible, going about three quarters of the way into the apple. Remove the core. Force the candle into the hollow center—it should be a snug fit.

Holding the two pieces of cord as if they were one, tie them in a bow around the base of the candle.

Make several Apple Candleholders and group them on a mantel (see photograph on page 160), on a sideboard or as a centerpiece.

MATERIALS

Red Delicious apple (Use unblemished apples that will stand solidly)

Apple corer

Straight or tapered candle, about ¾″ in diameter, 8″ long (You may cut down a longer candle to the correct size)

Gold cord, 2 pieces, each about 22″ long

*Apple Candleholder (page 159), Pinecone Candleholder (page 164), Small Heart
Wreaths (page 161): Design #1, top left, Design #2, top right, Design #3, top center*

Small Heart Wreaths

THE BASIC WREATH

1 Shape the chenille stem into a heart, as shown below, twisting the ends together at the bottom of the heart. NOTE: The top of the heart will be shaped to a more definite point later.

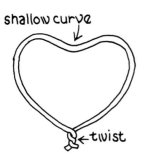

shallow curve

←twist

2 Cut two strips of sheet moss, each about 2″ wide and 8″ long, and cut a two-foot piece of thin wire. Beginning at the lower point, holding the strip of moss lengthwise and letting it overhang the lower point about 1″, wrap the moss *tightly* around the chenille. Wrap the wire firmly around the moss to secure it.

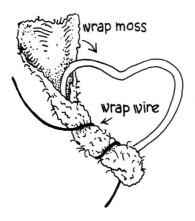

wrap moss

wrap wire

Continue wrapping the moss and wire all the way around the heart, working back to the beginning. When the first strip of moss is almost used up, overlap the second strip and keep going. If the wire runs out, cut two more feet and add it by twisting the beginning of the new piece to the end of the old piece.

At the lower point of the heart, overlap the ends of moss for 1″-2″, cutting off the excess. Wrap the wire around the ends of moss and twist the ends of wire together tightly on the back of the heart. Clip off any excess wire.

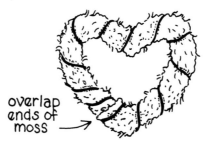

overlap
ends of
moss →

3 Shape the top part of the heart into a more definite point. With a scissors give the heart a little haircut—just a trim—to neaten it up. Clip off any bits of moss that are sticking out, so you can see the heart shape very clearly.

Tie the grosgrain ribbon to the top of the heart to form the loop.

MATERIALS FOR
THE BASIC
WREATH,
WITHOUT TRIMMING

Chenille stem (A chenille stem is simply a longer, plushier version of a pipe cleaner)

Sheet moss (This flat, irregularly shaped piece of dried moss is available at a florist or a florist's supply store. Brush some of the dirt away from the underside before trying to cut it)

Very thin wire, packed on a spool

Grosgrain ribbon, ⅛″ wide, one piece 15″ long for the loop

White glue

**MATERIALS
FOR DESIGN #1:**

Wired berries, 14-16 units

**Plaid taffeta ribbon, $\frac{5}{16}''$
wide, one piece 12" long for
the bow**

Wirecutter

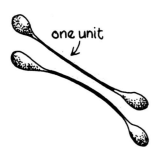

one unit

DESIGN #1

1 Tie the taffeta ribbon in a bow about 3"
wide with ends about $2\frac{1}{2}''$-3" long (see How
to Tie a Bow, page 17). Trim the ends on
the diagonal. Place the bow on the front of
the heart. Take two wired berry units and
form each into a U-shape. Wrap them
around the heart, one on each side of the
center knot of the bow. Twist the berries
and wire to secure the bow to the heart.

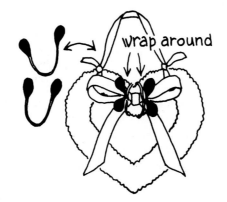

wrap around

2 With a wirecutter, clip 12-14 berry units
into shorter pieces, discarding the extra bits
of wire.

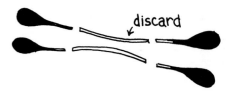

discard

  Dip the wire end of each berry in glue and
insert it in the moss around the bow as
shown in the color drawing.

DESIGN #2

1 Cut the dried statice into individual flowers, leaving a little green stem on each flower.

2 Cut a long piece of green thread and tie it to the left side of the heart as shown. Center one flower on the thread and wind the thread over the flower to secure it to the heart. Place a second flower overlapping the first. Bring the thread around and over the second flower to secure it.

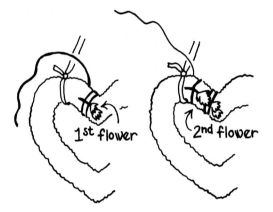

Continue in this manner, working down the left side of the heart, stopping at the lower point. Let the leftover thread hang free for now.

Go back to the upper point and repeat the process on the right side of the heart. At the lower point tie the two ends of thread together securely on the back of the heart and clip off any excess thread.

3 Tie the taffeta ribbon in a bow, snip the ends in points and glue the bow to the heart as shown in the photograph and drawing.

DESIGN #3:

1 Cut a piece of wire about 8″ long. Wrap one end several times around the "petals" at the base of one pinecone. The wire should be securely attached to the pinecone. Wrap the other end of the wire around a second pinecone, ending up with about 2½″-3″ of wire between the two pinecones. Repeat with a second pair of pinecones.

Twist the wired pinecones together with three berry units. Shape them into a "U" and twist them around the upper point of the heart to make a cluster.

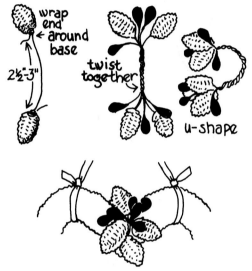

2 Strip the "petals" from the lower half of each of the remaining two to four pinecones, leaving the stems exposed. Dip each stem in glue and insert it into the moss at an upper curve of the heart, at the lower point, etc.

3 With a wirecutter, snip the remaining berry units into shorter pieces, discarding the extra bits of wire. Break off the stem of each dried flower to about ¾″ long.

Tuck these berries and flowers around the cluster and down the sides of the heart (as shown in the photograph and drawing) by dipping each wire or stem in glue and gently inserting it in the moss.

MATERIALS
FOR DESIGN #2:

Dried white statice flowers, 2 or 3 stems

Green thread

Plaid taffeta ribbon, $\frac{5}{16}$″ wide, one piece 10″ long for the bow

MATERIALS
FOR DESIGN #3:

6-8 tiny pinecones, each $\frac{1}{2}$″-$\frac{3}{4}$″ long

Wired berries (see drawing above), 7-9 units

35-40 small dried yellow flowers with rigid stems

Pinecone Candleholder

MATERIALS

Small pinecone, about 2″ high and 2″ wide (Check the photograph to see the type of cone best suited to this project)

Pliers, wirecutter

Styrofoam block, $\frac{7}{8}$″ thick, one piece 2″ × 2″ (For this project, buy a small sheet of $\frac{7}{8}$″-thick Styrofoam and cut it to size with a dovetail saw)

Small candle, about 3″ long, $\frac{1}{2}$″ in diameter

White glue

1 Use the pliers and wirecutter to pull and clip out the center top few "petals" from the pinecone to create a hollow for the candle.

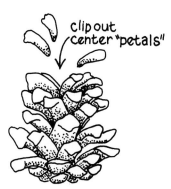

2 Press the bottom of the pinecone firmly into the center of the plastic foam block to make an indentation. Lift the pinecone and put glue into the indentation. Replace the

pinecone, fitting it back into the indentation. Let the glue dry.

3 Hold the bottom of the candle over the center of the pinecone. Apply the flame of a match to the bottom of the candle, letting drops of wax fall into the hollowed-out center of the pinecone. Quickly, while the drops of wax and the bottom of the candle are still warm and soft, press the candle into position in the center of the pinecone. The wax will act as glue to hold the candle in place. Try to keep the candle very straight. Let the wax cool and dry.

Wreaths with Natural Decorations

Start with an unadorned green wreath, store-bought or homemade, and make it special by trimming it with any of these natural decorations.

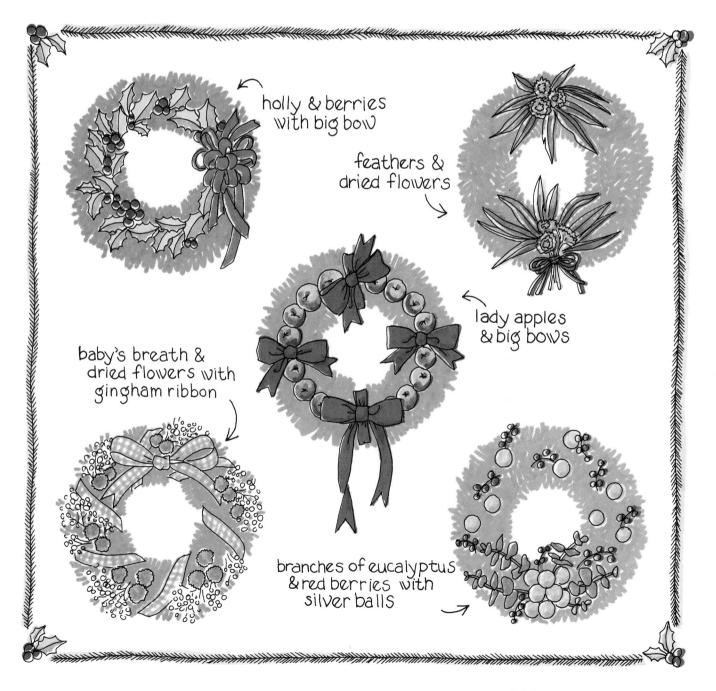

holly & berries with big bow

feathers & dried flowers

lady apples & big bows

baby's breath & dried flowers with gingham ribbon

branches of eucalyptus & red berries with silver balls

Index

Have BETTER HOMES AND GARDENS *magazine delivered to your door. For information, write to: Mr. Robert Austin, P.O. Box 4536, Des Moines, Iowa 50336.*